Learning BeagleBone

Learn how to love and care for your BeagleBone and teach it tricks

Hunyue Yau

[PACKT] open source ✽
PUBLISHING community experience distilled

BIRMINGHAM - MUMBAI

Learning BeagleBone

First published: December 2014

Production reference: 1191214

Published by Packt Publishing Ltd.
Livery Place
35 Livery Street
Birmingham B3 2PB, UK.

ISBN 978-1-78398-290-5

www.packtpub.com

Credits

Author
Hunyue Yau

Reviewers
Tobias Janke
Samuel de Ancos Martín

Commissioning Editor
Edward Gordon

Acquisition Editor
Sam Wood

Content Development Editor
Arun Nadar

Technical Editors
Indrajit A. Das
Shashank Desai

Copy Editors
Roshni Banerjee
Relin Hedly
Deepa Nambiar

Project Coordinator
Neha Bhatnagar

Proofreaders
Ameesha Green
Joanna McMahon

Indexer
Hemangini Bari

Graphics
Sheetal Aute
Valentina D'silva

Production Coordinator
Manu Joseph

Cover Work
Manu Joseph

About the Author

Hunyue Yau is an electrical engineer who graduated from the California Institute of Technology. He has worked with Linux since the early '90s, starting with the Soft Landing System. He created one of the first embedded Linux devices in 1996 with a custom-made distribution. He has worked on various products such as embedded Linux appliances, embedded BSD-based devices, and embedded Linux mobile devices. As an active member of the BeagleBoard community, he has volunteered at numerous community events, from Maker Faire to Google Summer of Code mentoring. Today, Hunyue synergizes his electrical engineering skills with embedded Linux software skills to provide turnkey embedded Linux consulting services through HY Research LLC (http://www.hy-research.com/), a company founded by him.

I would like to thank my wife, Betty, for supporting me while writing this book as well as the many members of the BeagleBoard community.

About the Reviewers

Tobias Janke lives in Northern Germany. He has been experimenting with computers and hardware since he learned to read. He realized several hardware projects and developed small applications at the age of 12. Then, with some more experience, he cofounded a local company that specializes in computer services and web design. As a hobby, he is working on computer-controlled hardware projects featuring embedded programming and sensors. He is currently developing a fully autonomous drone that is controlled by self-made hardware and software running on the BeagleBone Black.

Samuel de Ancos Martín got into his passion, software developing, from a very early age. Now he is an engineer and specializes in IoT development. He has been a part of the development team of Carriots, an IoT platform based in Spain, where he played an important part in its design, architecture, and development. He has also taken part in the prototype with free boards and integration hardware with the big manufacturers on the market. As a software developer and enthusiast, he has been working for more than 10 years on building Internet-oriented software. You can get more information about him on his website at http://deancos.com.

Samuel blogs occasionally at http://blog.deancos.com, in Spanish, about IoT and developing software in general. You can contact him on Twitter at @sdeancos or mail him at sdeancos@gmail.com.

I would like to thank my girlfriend and my family for supporting me while I was reviewing this magnificent book as well as all my colleagues who helped me grow as a better professional.

www.PacktPub.com

Support files, eBooks, discount offers, and more

For support files and downloads related to your book, please visit www.PacktPub.com.

Did you know that Packt offers eBook versions of every book published, with PDF and ePub files available? You can upgrade to the eBook version at www.PacktPub.com and as a print book customer, you are entitled to a discount on the eBook copy. Get in touch with us at service@packtpub.com for more details.

At www.PacktPub.com, you can also read a collection of free technical articles, sign up for a range of free newsletters and receive exclusive discounts and offers on Packt books and eBooks.

https://www2.packtpub.com/books/subscription/packtlib

Do you need instant solutions to your IT questions? PacktLib is Packt's online digital book library. Here, you can search, access, and read Packt's entire library of books.

Why subscribe?

- Fully searchable across every book published by Packt
- Copy and paste, print, and bookmark content
- On demand and accessible via a web browser

Free access for Packt account holders

If you have an account with Packt at www.PacktPub.com, you can use this to access PacktLib today and view 9 entirely free books. Simply use your login credentials for immediate access.

Table of Contents

Preface

The BeagleBone provides a vehicle for learning embedded devices. Regardless of whether you are a maker looking to embed a computer into your latest project or just interested in learning about embedded programming, the BeagleBone is the board to use. Unlike other low-cost controller boards, the BeagleBone is a fully fledged computer using current mobile technology made accessible for custom projects, prototypes, and learning. The BeagleBone can be programmed in almost any manner that a desktop or laptop Linux system can. Design material is openly available so projects can be independently manufactured.

This book goes through the basics of the BeagleBone boards along with exercises to guide a new user through the process of using the BeagleBone for the first time. It covers unboxing a new BeagleBone and basic configuration of a desktop or a laptop system so that the board can be programmed. For anyone who has previously used a microcontroller or has only programmed desktop systems, this book provides simple exercises using no more resources than what is on the board.

What this book covers

Chapter 1, Introducing the Beagle Boards, introduces you to the idea of the Beagle boards and also serves as a quick guide to the entire family of boards, as each board has unique features that may make one board more suitable than another. It goes on to unboxing your first BeagleBone and verifying whether it is running using a desktop or laptop system. It'll also take you through useful accessories for the BeagleBone.

Chapter 2, *Software in the BeagleBone*, introduces the software in the BeagleBone. It covers three aspects that include getting around the software that come with the board, getting precanned images onto the board, and building software for the board on the board. As part of this chapter, analogies to desktop software are provided.

Chapter 3, *Building an LED Flasher*, covers a basic introductory exercise of building a simple LED pattern flasher "product" using the LEDs on the BeagleBone, along with sample solutions. The entire example is doable with just the BeagleBone itself. The only other thing needed is a PC to interact with the board.

Chapter 4, *Refining the LED Flasher*, builds on the previous chapter and explains how to access the I2C bus. Again, no additional hardware is needed.

Chapter 5, *Connecting the BeagleBone to Mobile Devices*, looks at options to connect a BeagleBone to a mobile device, such as a phone using Bluetooth. It goes through different methods suitable for different types of mobile devices and the potential pitfalls of each method.

Chapter 6, *Recovering from the Mistakes*, covers possible mistakes that may cause the board to appear as dead. This chapter explains the process of attempting to recover from such mistakes. It also goes through a quick diagnostic process to determine whether the board is likely to be dead.

Chapter 7, *Interfacing with the BeagleBone*, takes you through the very basics of connecting simple hardware to the BeagleBone. It covers the basics of how to avoid damaging the board.

Chapter 8, *Advanced Software Topics*, covers more advanced ways of writing software for the BeagleBone. It provides guidance to help you go beyond what this book will cover.

Chapter 9, *Expansion Boards and Options*, explains what a cape is and the examples of off-the-shelf things that can be added. It also goes through the process of creating your own cape or even a basic expansion board.

Appendix A, *The Boot Process*, provides a slightly more detailed look at how a BeagleBone loads software while powering on. This is useful in finding rapid development methods or troubleshooting.

Appendix B, *Terms and Definitions*, provides background information on select terms used throughout the book for new BeagleBone users. These cover terms used both in this book and terms that may be encountered in the BeagleBone community.

What you need for this book

In order to go through this book, you should have a BeagleBone. Both the BeagleBone White and the BeagleBone Black are covered and can be used for the exercises. While the BeagleBone can be programmed in a standalone fashion, this book will focus on programming it through a desktop or a laptop system. As such, a desktop or a laptop running Windows or Linux is recommended. It is possible for a reader to use a Mac OS system, but this book assumes the user is familiar with Mac OS enough to bridge the gap between Mac OS and Windows or Linux. You should have some knowledge of getting around the laptop or desktop system.

Who this book is for

If you are not familiar with embedded Linux and would like to learn about it, this book is for you. This book is specifically targeting anyone who wants to use the BeagleBone as the vehicle for their learning; this includes makers who want to use the BeagleBone to control their latest product, or anyone who wants to learn to leverage current mobile technology, or someone who wants to move beyond simple microcontroller boards.

Conventions

In this book, you will find a number of styles of text that distinguish between different kinds of information. Here are some examples of these styles, and an explanation of their meaning.

Code words in text, database table names, folder names, filenames, file extensions, pathnames, dummy URLs, user input, and Twitter handles are shown as follows: "For Linux users, ssh root@192.168.7.2 will log you in to the board."

A block of code is set as follows:

```
$ ifconfig -a
....
eth1      Link encap:Ethernet  HWaddr 1c:ba:8c:95:18:a0
          inet addr:192.168.7.1  Bcast:192.168.7.3
Mask:255.255.255.252
          inet6 addr: fe80::1eba:8cff:fe95:18a0/64 Scope:Link
          UP BROADCAST RUNNING MULTICAST  MTU:1500  Metric:1
          RX packets:21 errors:0 dropped:0 overruns:0 frame:0
          TX packets:101 errors:0 dropped:0 overruns:0 carrier:0
          collisions:0 txqueuelen:1000
          RX bytes:5280 (5.2 KB)  TX bytes:21808 (21.8 KB)
....
```

Any command-line input or output is written as follows:

```
$ mount | grep sdb
/dev/sdb1 on /media/HYBOOT type vfat (rw,nosuid,nodev,uid=1000,gid=1000,s
hortname=mixed,dmask=0077,utf8=1,showexec,flush,uhelper=udisks)
$ sudo umount /dev/sdb1
```

New terms and **important words** are shown in bold. Words that you see on the screen, in menus or dialog boxes for example, appear in the text like this: "Enter the IP address in the **HostName** section."

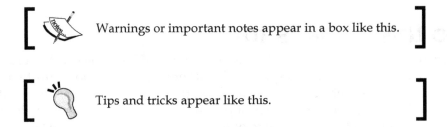

> Warnings or important notes appear in a box like this.

> Tips and tricks appear like this.

Reader feedback

Feedback from our readers is always welcome. Let us know what you think about this book—what you liked or disliked. Reader feedback is important for us as it helps us develop titles that you will really get the most out of.

To send us general feedback, simply e-mail feedback@packtpub.com, and mention the book's title in the subject of your message.

If there is a topic that you have expertise in and you are interested in either writing or contributing to a book, see our author guide at www.packtpub.com/authors.

Customer support

Now that you are the proud owner of a Packt book, we have a number of things to help you to get the most from your purchase.

Downloading the color images of this book

We also provide you with a PDF file that has color images of the screenshots/ diagrams used in this book. The color images will help you better understand the changes in the output. You can download this file from: `https://www.packtpub. com/sites/default/files/downloads/2905OS_ColoredImages.pdf`

Errata

Although we have taken every care to ensure the accuracy of our content, mistakes do happen. If you find a mistake in one of our books — maybe a mistake in the text or the code — we would be grateful if you could report this to us. By doing so, you can save other readers from frustration and help us improve subsequent versions of this book. If you find any errata, please report them by visiting `http://www.packtpub. com/submit-errata`, selecting your book, clicking on the **Errata Submission Form** link, and entering the details of your errata. Once your errata are verified, your submission will be accepted and the errata will be uploaded to our website or added to any list of existing errata under the Errata section of that title.

To view the previously submitted errata, go to `https://www.packtpub.com/books/ content/support` and enter the name of the book in the search field. The required information will appear under the **Errata** section.

Disclaimer

The BeagleBone is a sensitive electronic device and may be damaged by improper handling. Proper care should be taken during handling, development, and testing. Read all warnings in this book and in the BeagleBone documentation at `http:// beagleboard.org/`. Specifically, read and understand the SRM (Software Reference Manual). Do not attempt hardware interfacing without understanding limitations and specifications for the board and the associated components. The information in this book is provided on a best effort basis by the author. Software and hardware is constantly updated and, as such, it is possible for conflicting changes after the publication of this book. The author is not responsible for any damages.

Piracy

Piracy of copyright material on the Internet is an ongoing problem across all media. At Packt, we take the protection of our copyright and licenses very seriously. If you come across any illegal copies of our works, in any form, on the Internet, please provide us with the location address or website name immediately so that we can pursue a remedy.

Please contact us at copyright@packtpub.com with a link to the suspected pirated material.

We appreciate your help in protecting our authors, and our ability to bring you valuable content.

Questions

You can contact us at questions@packtpub.com if you are having a problem with any aspect of the book, and we will do our best to address it.

1
Introducing the Beagle Boards

This chapter will provide a background on the entire family of Beagle boards with brief highlights of what is unique about every member, such as things that favor one member over the other. This chapter will help you identify the Beagle boards that might have been mislabeled. The following topics will be covered here:

- What are Beagle boards
- How do they relate to other development boards
- BeagleBoard Classic
- BeagleBoard-xM
- BeagleBone White
- BeagleBone Black

The focus of this book will be on the BeagleBone subfamily and assumes that a BeagleBone board has been purchased.

The Beagle board family

The Beagle boards are a family of low-cost, open development boards that provide everyday students, developers, and other interested people with access to the current mobile processor technology on a path toward developing ideas. Prior to the invention of the Beagle family of boards, the available options to the user were primarily limited to either low-computing power boards, such as the 8-bit microcontroller-based Arduino boards, or dead-end options, such as repurposing existing products. There were even other options such as compromising the physical size or electrical power consumption by utilizing the nonmobile-oriented technology, for example, embedding a small laptop or desktop into a project. The Beagle boards attempt to address these points and more.

The Beagle board family provides you with access to the technologies that were originally developed for mobile devices, such as phones and tablets, and uses them to develop projects and for educational purposes. By leveraging the same technology for education, students can be less reliant on obsolete technologies. All this access comes affordably. Prior to the Beagle boards being available, development boards of this class easily exceeded thousands of dollars. In contrast, the initial Beagle board offering was priced at a mere 150 dollars!

The Beagle boards

The Beagle family of boards began in late 2008 with the original Beagle board. The original board has quite a few characteristics similar to all members of the Beagle board family. All the current boards are based on an ARM core and can be powered by a single 5V source or by varying degrees from a USB port. All boards have a USB port for expansion and provide direct access to the processor I/O for advance interfacing and expansion. Examples of the processor I/O available for expansion include **Serial Peripheral Interface (SPI)**, I2C, **pulse width modulation (PWM)**, and **general-purpose input/output (GPIO)**. The USB expansion path was introduced at an early stage providing a cheap path to add features by leveraging the existing desktop and laptop accessories.

All the boards are designed keeping the beginner in mind and, as such, are impossible to brick on software basis.

To brick a board is a common slang term that refers to damaging a board beyond recovery, thus, turning the board from an embedded development system to something as useful for embedded development as a brick.

This doesn't mean that they cannot be damaged electrically or physically. For those who are interested, the design and manufacturing material is also available for all the boards. The bill of material is designed to be available via distribution so that the boards themselves can be customized and manufactured even in small quantities. This allows projects to be manufactured if desired.

> Do not power up the board on any conductive surfaces or near conductive materials, such as metal tools or exposed wires. The board is fully exposed and doing so can subject your board to electrical damage. The only exception is a proper ESD mat designed for use with Electronics. The proper ESD mats are designed to be only conductive enough to discharge static electricity without damaging the circuits.

The following sections highlight the specifications for each member presented in the order they were introduced. They are based on the latest revision of the board. As these boards leverage mobile technology, the availability changes and the designs are partly revised to accommodate the available parts. The design information for older versions is available at http://www.beagleboard.org/.

BeagleBoard Classic

The initial member of the Beagle board family is the **BeagleBoard Classic** (**BBC**), which features the following specs:

- OMAP3530 clocked up to 720 MHz, featuring an ARM Cortex-A8 core along with integrated 3D and video decoding accelerators
- 256 MB of LPDDR (low-power DDR) memory with 512 MB of integrated (NAND) flash memory on board; older revisions had less memory
- USB OTG (switchable between a USB device and a USB host) along with a pure USB high-speed host-only port
- A low-level debug port accessible using a common desktop DB-9 adapter
- Analog audio in and out
- DVI-D video output to connect to a desktop monitor or a digital TV
- A full-size SD card interface
- A 28-pin general expansion header along with two 20-pin headers for video expansion
- 1.8V I/O

Only a nominal 5V is available on the expansion connector. Expansion boards should have their own regulator.

At the original release of the BBC in 2008, OMAP3530 was comparable to the processors of mobile phones of that time. The BBC is the only member to feature a full-size SD card interface. You can see the BeagleBoard Classic in the following image:

BeagleBoard-xM

As an upgrade to the BBC, the **BeagleBoard-xM** (**BBX**) was introduced later. It features the following specs:

- DM3730 clocked up to 1 GHz, featuring an ARM Cortex-A8 core along with integrated 3D and video decoding accelerators compared to 720 MHz of the BBC.

- 512 MB of LPDDR but no onboard flash memory compared to 256 MB of LPDDR with up to 512 MB of onboard flash memory.

- USB OTG (switchable between a USB device and a USB host) along with an onboard hub to provide four USB host ports and an onboard USB connected to the Ethernet interface. The hub and Ethernet connect to the same port as the high-speed port of the BBC. The hub allows low-speed devices to work with the BBX.

- A low-level debug port accessible with a standard DB-9 serial cable. An adapter is no longer needed.

- Analog audio in and out. This is the same analog audio in and out as that of the BBC.

- DVI-D video output to connect to a desktop monitor or a digital TV. This is the same DVI-D video output as used in the BBC.

- A microSD interface. It replaces the full-size SD interface on the BBC. The difference is mainly the physical size.

- A 28-pin expansion interface and two 20-pin video expansion interfaces along with an additional camera interface board. The 28-pin and two 20-pin interfaces are physically and electrically compatible with the BBC.

- 1.8V I/O.

 Only a nominal 5V is available on the expansion connector. Expansion boards should have their own regulator.

The BBX has a faster processor and added capabilities when compared to the BBC. The camera interface is a unique feature for the BBX and provides a direct interface for raw camera sensors. The 28-pin interface, along with the two 20-pin video interfaces, is electrically and mechanically compatible with the BBC. Mechanical mounting holes were purposely made backward compatible. Beginning with the BBX, boards were shipped with a microSD card containing the Angström Linux distribution.

The latest version of the kernel and bootloader are shared between the BBX and BBC. The software can detect and utilize features available on each board as the DM3730 and the OMAP3530 processors are internally very similar. You can see the BeagleBoard-xM in the following image:

BeagleBone

To simplify things and to bring in a low-entry cost, the BeagleBone subfamily of boards was introduced. While many concepts in this book can be shared with the entire Beagle family, this book will focus on this subfamily. All current members of BeagleBone can be purchased for less than 100 dollars.

BeagleBone White

The initial member of this subfamily is the **BeagleBone White (BBW)**. This new form factor has a footprint to allow the board itself to be stored inside an Altoids tin.

 The Altoids tin is conductive and can electrically damage the board if an operational BeagleBone without additional protection is placed inside it.

The BBW features the following specs:

- AM3358 clocked at up to 720 MHz, featuring an ARM Cortex-A8 core along with a 3D accelerator, an ARM Cortex-M3 for power management, and a unique feature — the **Programmable Real-time Unit Subsystem (PRUSS)**
- 256 MB of DDR2 memory
- Two USB ports, namely, a dedicated USB host and dedicated USB device
- An onboard JTAG debugger
- An onboard USB interface to access the low-level serial interfaces
- 10/100 MB Ethernet interfaces
- Two 46-pin expansion interfaces with up to eight channels of analog input
- 10-pin power expansion interface
- A microSD interface
- 3.3V digital I/O
- 1.8V analog I/O

As with the BBX, the BBW ships with the Angström Linux distribution. You can see the BeagleBone White in the following image:

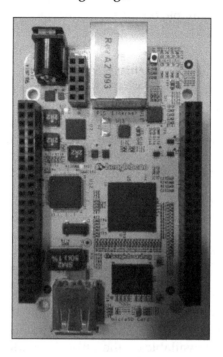

BeagleBone Black

Intended as a lower-cost version of the BeagleBone, the **BeagleBone Black (BBB)** features the following specs:

- AM3358 clocked at up to 1 GHz, featuring an ARM Cortex-A8 core along with a 3D accelerator, an ARM Cortex-M3 for power management, and a unique feature: the PRUSS. This is an improved revision of the same processor in the BBW.

- 512 MB of DDR3 memory compared to 256 MB of DDR2 memory on the BBW.

- 4 GB of onboard flash **embedded MMC (eMMC)** memory for the latest version compared to a complete lack of onboard flash memory on the BBW.

- Two USB ports, namely, a dedicated USB host and dedicated USB device.

- A low-level serial interface is available as a dedicated 6-pin header.

- 10/100 MB Ethernet interfaces.

- Two 46-pin expansion interfaces with up to eight channels of analog input.

- A microSD interface.
- A micro HDMI interface to connect to a digital monitor or a digital TV. A digital audio is available on the same interface. This is new to the BBB.
- 3.3V digital I/O.
- 1.8V analog I/O.

The overall mechanical form factor of the BBB is the same as that of the BBW. However, due to the added features, there are some slight electrical changes in the expansion interface. The power expansion header was removed to make room for added features. Unlike other boards, the BBB is shipped with a Linux distribution on the internal flash memory. Early revisions shipped with Angström Linux and later revisions shipped with Debian Linux as an attempt to simplify things for new users.

Unlike the BBW, the BBB does not provide an onboard JTAG debugger or an onboard USB to serial converter. Both these features were provided by a single chip on the BBW and were removed from the BBB for cost reasons. JTAG debugging is possible on the BBB by soldering a connector to the back of the BBB and using an external debugger. Access to the serial port on the BBB is provided by a serial header.

This book will focus solely on the BeagleBone subfamily (BBW and BBB). The difference between them will be noted where applicable. It should be noted that for more advanced projects, the BBC/BBX should be considered as they offer additional unique features that are not available on the BBW/BBB. Most concepts learned on the BBB/BBW boards are entirely applicable to the BBC/BBX boards. You can see the BeagleBone Black in the following image:

Summary of the Beagle board family

At the moment, there are four members in the Beagle board family, each with unique features but all having the common goal of making technology accessible. The BBC and BBX share a similar expansion connector and offer media-handling capabilities. The BBW and BBB share a similar expansion connector and offer a low cost while using the PRUSS for custom peripherals and real-time options. While all the boards offer a good educational experience, this book will focus on the BBW and BBB.

Congratulations on selecting a BeagleBone board

Depending on the BeagleBone you have purchased, the getting started process is slightly different. Assuming that you have purchased a new board from an authorized distributor with included accessories, we will now assemble it.

 Using some of the accessories, namely, the SD card reader and the mains adapter, the BBB and the BBW can be restored to the factory state by following the instructions in *Chapter 2, Software in the BeagleBone*. A mains adapter also known as a DC power adapter or an AC adapter is required.

We'll first go through what's included and then a few very useful accessories to have.

 At the time of writing this book, there are authorized branded boards being introduced at http://beagleboard.org/.

Unboxing and powering up your BeagleBone

For the BBB, the box will contain the BBB board in an ESD-safe protective bag (a silver-colored bag), and a USB cable with a mini connector on one end and a standard USB A connector on the other.

 The BeagleBone boards are sensitive to static electricity; hence, store the board in the protective ESD bag when not in use.

You can see the BeagleBone Black board with its contents in the following image:

For the BBW, the contents are similar except that it also contains a microSD card along with a microSD to full-size SD adapter. For the purposes of this book, the SD adapter is not needed but more advanced uses, such as recovery of the board, might require the adapter. You can see the BeagleBone White board with its contents in the following image:

In order to power up the BeagleBone for the first time, a desktop or a laptop with a USB port should be available. If possible, do not use an external hub. If you must use a hub, be sure to use a self-power hub (a hub that has its own power supply). The board as shipped is designed to work with most desktop/laptops. However, there are some corner case configurations, which we will address later. The board has been tested with systems that run Linux, Windows, and Mac OS. The configuration is generally the easiest with a Linux system but it is not necessary.

This book will focus on Linux and Windows. The Mac OS configuration should be similar. The overall process is described at http://beagleboard.org/static/beaglebone/latest/README.htm and http://beagleboard.org/Getting%20Started.

For the BBW users, the microSD card should be inserted at this point prior to connecting the mini USB cable; the BBB users can proceed to connecting the mini USB cable.

The microSD card only fits in one way. If it does not appear to fit, remove and flip it over. Do not force the card.

Regardless of the operating system, the first step is to plug the mini USB cable into the BeagleBone.

The mini USB connector is at the bottom of the board under the LEDs, next to the big silver RJ45 jack. The USB port is marked as **USB**.

When the BeagleBone is powered on from the machine, a blue power LED will immediately light. If the LED doesn't glow or if it just blinks on briefly, it is possible that your machine might fall in the corner case category and you might need the power adapter as described later. The earlier URL mentions additional steps but other steps such as upgrading to the latest image are optional. Similarly, configuring the board for serial access is also optional.

The exercises in this book should work fine with the shipping images. An image here refers to the system software. Usually, updating the system software will add new features and fix bugs. The system software shipped with the board should be enough for the exercises in this book. So, you can use it to develop an understanding of the BeagleBone before diving into its upgrades. In *Chapter 2*, *Software in the BeagleBone*, we will look at the system software in more detail. You can see how the USB cables connect to the BeagleBone Black and BeagleBone White in the following image:

The standard BeagleBone software at the time of writing this book provides two standard USB functions for the BBB and one additional function for the BBW out of the box. They are as follows:

- **USB mass storage**: This is a standard USB way of providing access to a storage device. Other examples of UMS devices are the USB thumb drives; most include drivers to support UMS.

- **USB Ethernet**: This is one of the many methods of providing a virtual-network interface with USB. The configuration supports the **Remote Network Driver Interface Specification (RNDIS)** method so that it can work out of the box with Windows without sacrificing the Linux compatibility. The net result is a virtual-network interface that appears on both Linux and Windows.

- **(BBW only) FTDI serial adapter**: This is a combination serial port adapter connected to a serial console and a JTAG interface. It is implemented as an additional piece of hardware on the BBW. This hardware is combined with the preceding two functions implemented by the Linux system running on the BeagleBone with an onboard hub. The exercises in this book will not use this part of the BBW.

The Windows configuration

In order to access the BeagleBone from Windows, a few basic drivers need to be installed. The latest drivers can be downloaded from `http://beagleboard.org/ getting-started`. A version of the driver is available directly from the BeagleBone. Shortly after plugging in the USB cable, a USB drive will appear on the desktop/ laptop. Navigate to the drive. There will be a folder named `Drivers`, and inside it, there will a folder named `Windows`. Run the installer appropriate for your version of Windows (64 bit or 32 bit). There might be some security warnings about driver signing.

Depending on your version of Windows, you might need to restart/reboot. Afterwards, a network device will appear.

> If you choose to use an emulated environment, note that the BeagleBone will appear as a composite device. You might need to assign multiple devices to the emulated environment. For Mac OS users, there are native Mac OS drivers available at `http://beagleboard.org/ getting-started`. The BBW users will see two potentially added USB devices, namely, a FTDI device and a hub.

The Linux configuration

For the exercises in this book, no additional drivers are needed in most distributions. Most distributions will recognize the virtual Ethernet device provided by the system software on the BeagleBone. When the BeagleBone is plugged in, it will provide a composite device that offers a virtual Ethernet and a mass storage device. Unless specifically disabled, the Linux kernel will recognize and attach appropriate drivers. You can verify that the Beagle board is accessible by looking at the new network interface. This can be done by looking at the output of the following `ifconfig` command before and after plugging in the Beagle board:

```
$ ifconfig -a
....
eth1      Link encap:Ethernet  HWaddr 1c:ba:8c:95:18:a0
          inet addr:192.168.7.1  Bcast:192.168.7.3
Mask:255.255.255.252
          inet6 addr: fe80::1eba:8cff:fe95:18a0/64 Scope:Link
          UP BROADCAST RUNNING MULTICAST  MTU:1500  Metric:1
          RX packets:21 errors:0 dropped:0 overruns:0 frame:0
          TX packets:101 errors:0 dropped:0 overruns:0 carrier:0
          collisions:0 txqueuelen:1000
          RX bytes:5280 (5.2 KB)  TX bytes:21808 (21.8 KB)
....
```

The network device for the BeagleBone will appear as shown in the preceding code. It will use the `192.168.7.1` address. Depending on the distribution, the name of the network device might appear as a device with an `eth` or a USB prefix.

If the network device does not appear as described here, your distribution might need additional drivers installed. Check with your distribution's documentation or support community for details on how to enable support for a CDC Ethernet device.

Useful PC software for your BeagleBone

In order to follow the exercises in this book, you will need to have a few basic pieces of software. The basic exercises will require an SSH client to be installed on your desktop or laptop where the BeagleBone is connected to. The pieces of software required are as follows:

- For Windows users, PuTTY is available from `http://www.putty.org/`.

- For Linux users, OpenSSH or dropbear is often installed by default. You can verify this by typing `ssh` in the shell prompt. If you get a help message about the `ssh` usage, you should be ready.

- For Mac OS users, MacSSH can be downloaded for free from `http://www.macssh.com/ssh_down.html`.

For more advanced exercises, a web browser is needed. The exercises should work with any web browser. However, the getting started pages might not work correctly in Internet Explorer. It is strongly recommended that you use another browser, such as Firefox.

Accessing the BeagleBone

As shipped, the BeagleBone provides a web server and an SSH server. As a first test, enter `http://192.168.7.2/` and the following web page (served by the BeagleBone) will appear:

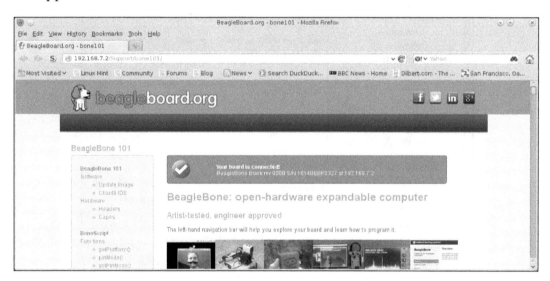

Congratulations! You now have a working BeagleBone!

As all the exercises in this book require shell access, the next step will be to attempt to access the BeagleBone by SSH. The following are a few specifications:

- For Linux users, `ssh root@192.168.7.2` will log you in to the board.

- For Windows users, run PuTTY, connect to `192.168.7.2`, and use `root` as the username to log in to the board. You will then see the following screenshot. Enter the IP address in the **HostName** section. After clicking on **Open**, you will be prompted to enter the username (`root`). If you are prompted for a password, just press *Enter*.

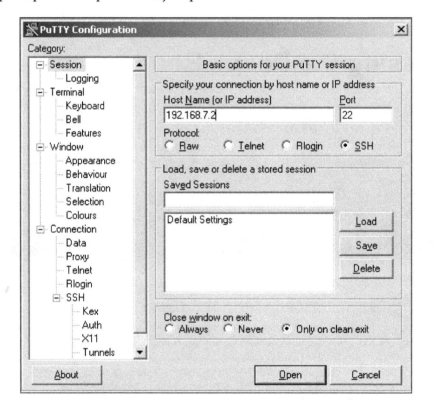

For both Linux and Windows users, you will be asked to confirm the SSH key for the BeagleBone. Enter `YES` when asked.

If you successfully log in to the board, you are ready for the exercises.

Useful accessories

There are a few accessories that can be very helpful when accessing the BeagleBone boards.

The mains power adapter

The first and possibly the most helpful accessory is a 5V wall outlet/mains power adapter. This will allow you to power the BeagleBone from the wall outlet instead of drawing power from a USB port. While the board can be powered by the USB port, if you want to do anything that requires more than the minimal amount of power, a 5V wall out/mains power adapter is strongly recommended. If capes or expansion boards are installed, the amount of power can easily exceed what is available from the USB port. These adapters are available from a variety of sources. The specifications you are looking for are as follows:

- Regulated 5V power supply
- 1 to 2A of current
- A female barrel connector with 2.1 mm inner diameter and 5.5 mm outer diameter with the center positive

This might also be necessary if your laptop or desktop strictly enforces the USB standard, which only provides 100mA of power initially and a maximum of 500mA.

An SD card reader and microSD cards

A USB SD or microSD card reader is one of the other important accessories. Numerous images and software upgrades are available for download over the Internet. More importantly, if you ever need to restore the BeagleBone to a factory state, such as after a mistake, an SD card reader and a microSD card are absolutely essential as this is done by a software image download. To use these images, a means of writing to the microSD card is needed. The software installation process is detailed in *Chapter 2, Software in the BeagleBone*. Almost any card reader will work; however, it is strongly advised to get the one that is USB 2.0 high-speed capable. This is because most images are relatively large and can take a while with a slower device.

In addition, as a companion to the SD card reader, a fast microSD card is highly desirable. For the BBW, the microSD card as shipped is functional but it is often a very slow card. The microSD cards are rated by a class system. Getting a reliable high-speed microSD card can help improve the performance considerably for the BBW. For the BBB, this is less important but it can help accelerate updates.

If you do not have a microSD to full-size SD card adapter, be sure that you purchase one. The microSD cards are often (but not always) sold in a package that includes the adapter. Alternatively, you can buy a card reader that can directly take microSD cards.

A serial debug cable

For the BBB, a USB to serial cable can be very helpful in debugging the system or troubleshooting an apparently non-booting board. The FTDI TTL-232R-3V3 cable, available from **Future Technology Devices International (FTDI)**, Digi-Key, and other distributors will provide access to the low-level debug serial port. This cable plugs in to a 6-pin header on the BBB. Pay attention to the triangle indicating pin one. For the BBW, this functionality is built-in but a driver might be needed depending on the operating system used in the desktop/laptop. You can see the connector for the serial adapter in the following image (pin one is marked by the white dot):

This cable converts the 3.3V UART signal into a USB signal accessible from the desktop/laptop. Other means of doing the same exists but their discussion is outside the scope of this book. See the **System Reference Manual (SRM)** and/or schematics for details.

A digital multimeter

A **digital multimeter (DMM)** is an extremely useful and relatively inexpensive accessory for the BeagleBone.

 For people not familiar with a basic DMM, a DMM allows you to measure voltage, resistance, and current. For most of our purposes, we are primarily looking at the voltage. The very basic DMM is sufficient for most of our purposes.

DMMs provide a lot of insights if there are any problems. Exercises in this book do not require a multimeter, but it can be very helpful in debugging. Power problems and examining signals are just some of the things a DMM can help us with. The BeagleBone boards provide analog inputs and the DMM provides a way to verify these analog signals. Even for digital signals, the DMM can provide a basic insight in signals not connected to LEDs, which are most of them. You can see a basic, low-cost DMM in the following image (the probes are connected and the function is selected by the rotary switch in the center):

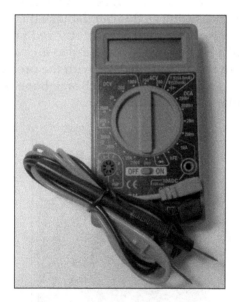

A typical, basic DMM will have two test leads connected, a black one and a red one, with a very sharp point on the end.

 Be careful and do not poke yourself or anyone else with the leads.

Typically, DMMs will have a rotary switch to select the measurement function or range. For most of our purposes, we will be measuring signals between 0 and 5V. So, in the case of the pictured DMM, the 20V setting marked by **20** in the upper-left area marked as **DCV** for the DC voltage will work.

Using the DMM on the BBB

To measure a signal on the BBB, first select the appropriate voltage measurement range. For the preceding DMM, a 20V range is the most appropriate as the BBB uses 3.3V for most signals.

 Do not attempt to measure anything you don't know the range of, as this can be very dangerous.

After selecting the range, connect the black probe to a reference point. Electrically, this is the ground. The ground signal is available on the exposed parts of the BeagleBone mounting hole, on the pins labeled as ground on the expansion header, or on the metal part of the Ethernet or RJ45 connector. Be very careful not to touch anything else with the probe while measuring as this can damage the BeagleBone. After connecting the black probe to the ground, connect the red probe to the signal being measured. An example of a signal you can measure as an exercise is the power line. Again, pay attention not to touch anything else with the probe to avoid shorting out signals. You can see a few ground points on the BeagleBone Black in the following image (the BBW has similar ground points):

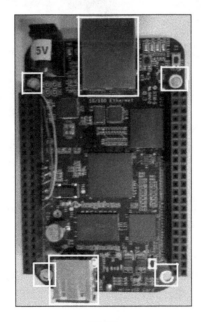

If you need a signal to practice measurement or to familiarize yourself with using a DMM, consider measuring the power supply signals on the expansion connector. This is worth repeating; be careful when measuring as accidentally shorting the signal to an adjacent pin or to anything else on the BeagleBone can permanently damage your board! You can locate power supply signals by referring to the SRMs section on the expansion connector pin outs. The connector P9 contains most of the power signals. On P9, you will find signals such as DC_3.3V, SYS_5V, and VDD_5V. The DC_3.3V signal should measure around 3.3V if the board is powered on and working correctly. VDD_5V is powered on only via a 5V barrel connector. SYS_5V is powered when the BeagleBone is powered on either by a 5V barrel connector or a USB connector.

The following are the two main strategies to measure the signal:

- **Measure at the top side**: The signals for the expansion connector are on the female connectors, as shown in the preceding image. You will need some kind of thin wire that fits the connector. In addition, if you later have an expansion board or a cape connected, the connectors themselves might be obscured. While some expansion boards might carry the signals through the expansion board themselves, they are not required to do so. This is especially true for the nonpower signals.

- **Measure on the bottom side of the board**: This has the advantage of allowing direct probing with a greater risk of shorting to adjacent signals. If you are careful, this provides the easiest access to the signals on the BeagleBone.

If you are unsure or trying to measure the signals on the BeagleBone for the first time, it is a good idea to seek help from someone knowledgeable to confirm whether your connections are correct and that you have not accidentally shorted out the signals.

Wireless interfacing accessories

For folks who want to attempt to interface the BeagleBone wirelessly, a Bluetooth USB adapter or a Wi-Fi USB adapter might be useful. Refer to the mailing list at http://www.beagleboard.org/Community/Forums for possible supported Wi-Fi adapters, as they will vary over time. This book will not discuss the Wi-Fi configuration but in *Chapter 5, Connecting the BeagleBone to Mobile Devices*, we will go through a few issues faced while connecting the BeagleBone to a mobile device, such as a phone.

Summary

In this chapter, we looked at the Beagle board offerings and a few unique features of each offering. Then, we went through the process of setting up a BeagleBone board and understood the basics to access it from a laptop/desktop. By verifying access to the BeagleBone via a web browser and a command line, we built a foundation for the exercises in the upcoming chapters.

With a new board, we also went through a list of some very useful accessories. With the exception of the power adapter for a few people with laptops/desktops that strictly enforce power limits, none of the accessories are required for the exercises in this book. You can proceed through the rest of the book while the accessories are ordered.

In the next chapter, we will look at system software in the BeagleBone along with the process of flashing a new image onto the BeagleBone.

Software in the BeagleBone

Now that you have unboxed your BeagleBone and have the basic accessories to connect to another machine, we'll look at the software in the BeagleBone. First, we'll look at the available distributions for the BeagleBone and then go over how to get these distributions onto the BeagleBone. To install a distribution, you need an SD card reader as mentioned in the previous chapter. Finally, we'll look at how to get your own software in the BeagleBone.

 A Linux distribution (often known as distro) is a collection of software composed of the Linux kernel and support pieces that provides a user interface.

If you have a new BeagleBone board and the accessories have not arrived but you are just anxious to get started, you can skip this chapter and move on to the next. Come back to this chapter when you need to change the software, either to try something different or for recovery purposes.

In this chapter, we will cover the following topics:

- System software in the BeagleBone
- BeagleBone distributions
- Angström and Debian Linux distributions for the BeagleBone
- Distribution installation on the BeagleBone from Windows and Linux hosts
- Bootable images versus flasher images
- Nonsystem software in the BeagleBone

System software in the BeagleBone

This book will focus solely on running a Linux-based software in the BeagleBone. It is possible to run almost any ARM-based software in the BeagleBone but this is outside the scope of the book.

 The examples of a few other distributions can be found at http://beagleboard.org/projects. This is not an exhaustive list.

The Linux-based system software comes in different flavors, commonly referred to as distribution. Linux by itself strictly refers to a core piece known as the kernel. A distribution takes the Linux kernel, configures things in a specific way, and then adds other system software pieces.

 Linux provides protection between different pieces of software to increase the overall system's robustness. This is done by having a supervisor or a privileged portion and an underprivileged portion. The privileged portion resides mostly in the kernel. The unprivileged portion is typically referred to as userland pieces. Userland pieces are, by default, isolated from each other and obtain services from the kernel.

Each distribution has its own style of configuration and policies. However, for basic things, they have a lot in common. Typical reasons to favor a particular distribution on the BeagleBone would be flexibility in configuring the system for a particular need, or compatibility with the existing legacy pieces. For beginners, easy access to the configuration and prior experience with a distribution is often another reason. However, as one becomes more familiar with the BeagleBone and Linux, other reasons will dominate the choice of distributions.

Distributions on the BeagleBone

The BeagleBone can run many different distributions similar to those available for desktops and laptops. However, the BeagleBone is shipped with two specific distributions, namely, Angström and Debian. Both the flavors are available in an easy-to-load format specifically for the BeagleBone.

The Angström Linux distribution

Angström has supported every Beagle board available since the beginning. The BeagleBone White is shipped with a microSD card that contains Angström. Early revisions of the BeagleBone Black were shipped pre-installed with the Angström. A quick overview of Angström (`http://www.angstrom-distribution.org/`) is as follows:

- Angström is built with OpenEmbedded and provides a lot of configuration flexibility

- Angström is more commonly used with embedded devices and is a little bit different from what people might be used to on the desktop/laptop

- The entire image can be locally built to give you an image with all the specific sources used in the image

- Building a package that isn't already set up for Angström requires writing a recipe, which can be daunting for new users

The Debian Linux distribution

Debian has been ported with the help of the community. Up until the latest version of the BeagleBone Black, this has been largely an alternative distribution for folks who want something much closer to a typical desktop or laptop distribution. Also lumped together under Debian is the popular Debian-derived distribution, Ubuntu. A quick overview of Debian (`https://www.debian.org/ports/arm/`) is as follows:

- Debian shares packages with the standard ARM Debian port. The primary difference is that the kernel, bootloader, and low-level setup are specific to the BeagleBone.

- For most part, Debian is the same as Debian on desktops or laptops. This brings some level of familiarity for new users.

- Despite the difference in the nature of things done on a BeagleBone versus desktops, there will still be quite a few differences, such as the way in which the system boots and the support for the USB device mode. A BeagleBone that runs Debian will often be performing more hardware-related things than a desktop or laptop.

- Debian is only pre-installed with the latest revision of the BeagleBone Black. All other revisions will require this to be explicitly loaded.

Installing a distribution in the BeagleBone

The process of installing a distribution in the BeagleBone differs between the White and Black versions. The BBW does not have a built-in flash memory, unlike the BBB. The process of installing a distribution on the BBW is a matter of writing the image onto the microSD card and booting from it. In contrast, the BBB has an onboard memory to which you can copy the files. However, the BBB also offers a microSD slot. This provides the BBB user with an option to test out a distribution using the microSD card while keeping the stock image intact, similar to how a BBW is set up.

Before beginning, make sure that the following items are available:

- A blank microSD card at least 1 GB or bigger. The size needed depends on the image; internal flash on a BBB is 2 GB on older revisions and 4 GB on newer revisions. The card does not need to be blank but the contents will be erased in the process, so make sure that there is nothing on the card that you want to keep.
- An SD (or microSD) card reader/writer for the desktop/laptop. Make sure that this is functional prior to beginning.
- A barrel power supply, as described in the previous chapter, is highly recommended to flash a BBB's onboard memory, as writing to flash often draws more power than a USB port can provide.

Obtaining the image

Regardless of the BeagleBone or distribution, the first step is to download the image, which can be found at http://beagleboard.org/latest-images.

There are two types of images found on this page. The first type of image is a generic, ready-to-run image suitable for use on the BBW or on the microSD slot of a BBB without changing the contents of the onboard flash. The second type of image is a flasher image that will install the distribution onto the onboard flash of a BBB. The flasher images cannot be used on a BBW as it lacks the onboard flash.

The images on the web page are compressed with 7-Zip. For Windows users who do not have a 7-Zip decompressor, it can be downloaded from http://www.7-zip.org/download.html.

For Linux, there are several options; one of them is xz-utils. On a Debian/Ubuntu system, this can be installed using the following command:

```
sudo apt-get install xz-utils
```

For BBB owners looking to try a different distribution, you will need to decide whether you want to overwrite the contents of the onboard flash or not. If you do not wish to overwrite the existing contents of the onboard flash, download the general image (the same image as that of the BBW); otherwise, download the flasher image.

Once a choice (if any) is made, download the image onto the laptop/desktop and then decompress it using the preceding tools.

Windows users

Assuming that you have installed the graphical version of 7-Zip correctly using the defaults, you should have a 7-Zip group in your Start menu. Also, there should be an application named 7-Zip File Manager. Start it and select the downloaded image. Decompress it with the **Extract** option at the top of the page. When prompted, enter a place to extract the contents to, as shown in the following screenshot:

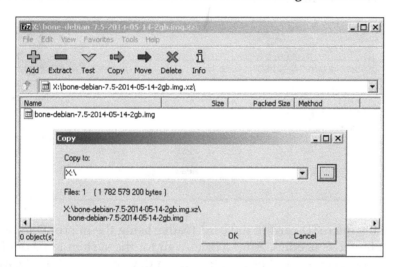

Remember where you decompress it to, as that path will be needed to write the image.

Linux users

Assuming that you have installed the `xz-utils` package, you should be able to decompress the image by running the following command:

```
unxz -d downloaded_imagename.xz
```

```
$ unxz -d bone-debian-7.5-2014-05-14-2gb.img.xz
```

Writing the image

The process of writing out the image depends on the type of desktop/laptop and the particular BeagleBone.

Windows users

Windows users will need an image-writing utility, such as Win32DiskImager, which can be found at `http://sourceforge.net/projects/win32diskimager/files/latest/download`.

After installation, a new application, Win32DiskImager, should appear in your Start menu under **Image Writer** if installed using the defaults. To use Win32DiskImager, follow these steps:

1. Start Win32DiskImager and you will see the following screenshot:

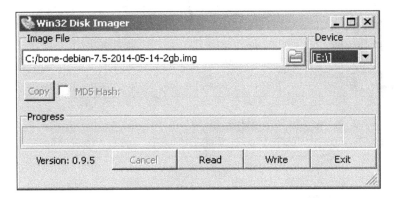

2. Insert the microSD card in the card reader using the microSD to full-size SD card adapter as needed. After a brief wait for the system to recognize the card reader, you should be able to select a device. Select the SD card reader device. The device selection is found on the upper-right side of the dialog box. It will only show the valid devices.

3. Select the image file you decompressed previously by clicking on the blue folder icon to the left-hand side of the device selector.

> The value generated by checking the **MD5 Hash** option will not match the value from the downloaded site. MD5 Hash (also known as the MD5 sum or simply as MD5) from the website is for the compressed file only. The process of decompressing the file will change MD5 Hash.

4. Click on the **Write** button at the bottom. You will be asked to confirm the target device. If you are unsure at this point, seek assistance to avoid data corruption. Confirm that you wish to continue. After confirming, the area labeled **Progress** will become active, and you will see a percent value along with a graphical progress bar, as shown in the following screenshot. Writing to the microSD card can take a while, depending on the type of card and reader you are using.

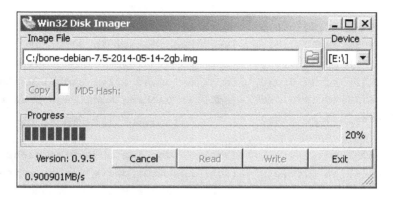

The write process will be complete once the progress indicates **100%**.

 The active progress bar and the percentage value are on the right. This indicates the write process has started successfully.

Linux users

For Linux users, most distributions include tools to write the image. The first step is to identify the name of the SD card reader.

 An error here can corrupt the desktop/laptop system.

For users using an USB-connected SD card reader, follow these steps:

1. Open a terminal on the desktop/laptop.

2. Insert the microSD card into the card reader using the microSD to full-size SD card adapter as needed. Connect the card reader to the machine. Wait a brief moment to allow the machine to recognize the card reader.

3. Run dmesg again in the terminal and note the last few lines or optionally run

dmesg | tail -10.

Piping a command in the tail is a convenient way to show only the last few lines. See the man page for details.

The name of the device will be in the form of sdX, where X is a lowercase letter from a to z. Note the name here:

```
$ dmesg | tail -10
[1001582.210640] sd 30:0:0:0: >[sdb] Write Protect is off
[1001582.210653] sd 30:0:0:0: >[sdb] Mode Sense: 4b 00 00 08
[1001582.210969] sd 30:0:0:0: >[sdb] No Caching mode page present
[1001582.210981] sd 30:0:0:0: >[sdb] Assuming drive cache: write through
[1001582.216573] sd 30:0:0:0: >[sdb] No Caching mode page present
[1001582.216586] sd 30:0:0:0: >[sdb] Assuming drive cache: write through
[1001582.225289]   sdb: sdb1 sdb2
[1001582.226833] sd 30:0:0:0: >[sdb] No Caching mode page present
[1001582.226846] sd 30:0:0:0: >[sdb] Assuming drive cache: write through
[1001582.226856] sd 30:0:0:0: >[sdb] Attached SCSI removable disk
```

In the preceding example, the line sdb: sdb1 sdb2 identifies the SD card reader as sdb with two partitions.

For users using an SD card reader built in a laptop, follow these steps (the name can depend on how you are attached to the system):

1. Make sure that there is no SD card inserted. If there is one, eject/remove the card after following the process normally done to remove the card.

2. Open a terminal.

3. Run dmesg and note the last few lines.

4. Insert an SD card into the card reader.

5. Run dmesg again.

The output will be similar to using a USB card reader but the name might differ. There are two common forms of the device name, depending on how it is connected. One is the device name sdX, where X is a lowercase letter, or it can be named mmcblkN, where N is a number, that is, mmcblk0. Note the name here.

If the name is still unclear, seek assistance. For the preceding examples, we will assume that the device name is sdb.

Depending on your system configuration, the SD card might be automatically mounted. Writing a new image to a mounted card can result in an unexpected behavior. To check whether an image is mounted, enter the following command in the Terminal window:

```
$ mount | grep sdb
```

Replace sdb with the name of your device. If that line returns a line, you will need to unmount it as follows:

```
$ sudo umount /dev/sdb1
```

The /dev/sdb1 value should be replaced with the name found in the beginning of the line, as shown in the following command:

```
$ mount | grep sdb
/dev/sdb1 on /media/HYBOOT type vfat (rw,nosuid,nodev,uid=1000,gid=1000,
shortname=mixed,dmask=0077,utf8=1,showexec,flush,uhelper=udisks)
$ sudo umount /dev/sdb1
```

While the name of the device is sdc or mmcblk0, the name shown in the first column might include an additional number (such as sdc1) or the letter p and a number (such as mmcblk0p1); include the number in the umount command. To write the image onto the SD card, type the following command:

```
sudo dd if=/image of=/dev/sdc bs=1M
```

This command might take a while to execute, depending on the speed of the SD card and the size of the image. This command does not provide updates, so be patient. For more details on the dd command, refer to the man page for dd.

Booting the image

Now that the downloaded image is written to the SD card, the card is ready to be used. If you have a BBB and would like to write the image to the onboard flash, make sure that you have downloaded a flasher image. For all other uses, make sure that you have downloaded a non-flasher image.

For the BBB users, if you have a USB serial cable, plug it in and configure your terminal software. This will provide useful feedback. For the BBW users, a similar output is available using the built-in, integrated USB serial adapter. The serial port will provide hints if the new image does not boot correctly.

To boot the image, follows these steps:

1. Disconnect the power to the BeagleBone. This includes disconnecting both the USB cable and the barrel power connection if one is used.

2. Insert the microSD card into the slot in the BBB or BBW.

3. For the BBB users only, locate the user button. You will need to depress and hold the button for the next step.

> This step only applies to the BBB. The BBW does not have a user button. The user button is used to select between booting from an onboard flash and the microSD slot. Depending on what is currently on the BBB's onboard flash, it might appear to boot from the microSD card due to some secondary checks. Holding down the user button while the power is first applied is necessary to ensure that the only software running is from the microSD card. The user button on the BBB forces the system to attempt to boot from the microSD media instead of the onboard flash. The user button is only checked on power up. It is not checked on reset! For non-flasher images, the user button can be released at this point. See the next section for flasher images.

4. Apply the power by connecting the barrel connector (if used) or the USB cable. The 5V power LED should light up. You can release the user button approximately 20 seconds after the power LED is on. These 20 seconds are longer than some sources suggest to give other pieces of software a chance to see the user button depressed.

If you have downloaded a non-flasher image, such as an image intended for both the BBW and BBB, the system is ready at this point.

Flasher images

For the BBB, there is an option to flash an OS onto the onboard flash. This same option can be used to restore a BBB to a factory condition if the onboard flash is corrupted due to experiments or if a BBB is sourced second hand. Unless you have the USB to serial cable, there will be minimal feedback provided through the flashing process.

> The flashing process can take up to an hour depending on the image. Do not power down or remove the microSD card while the BBB is flashing. This can potentially damage the board.

Unlike non-flasher images, the user button should be held down until all four LEDs next to the Ethernet briefly light up.

> Holding down the user button for the additional time is to let the flasher image know you really want to flash. The flashing process on older images ends with an automatic system reboot, which normally would not have the user button held down. This avoids a flashing loop.

The completion of the flashing process is indicated by the same four LEDs next to the Ethernet staying on. At this point, the BBB can be powered down manually. The system will not reboot automatically on most newer images.

Nonsystem software in the BeagleBone

After the BeagleBone boots the kernel and allows you to log in, the system is ready to run the nonsystem software. This software runs in an unprivileged level, so bugs here are unlikely to crash the entire system. This software is typically what makes the BeagleBone specific to a task. Later on in this book, we will write this type of software as an exercise to familiarize ourselves with the BeagleBone. The line between the system software and nonsystem software can be unclear as most distribution includes a vast library of applications, either installed or easily installable with a few commands. The exact process depends on the distribution. For Angström users, this is done using the opkg command. For Debian users, this is done either by apt-get or dpkg just like on a desktop machine.

For a lot of BeagleBone users, the software library offered by distributions is commonly just a foundation to build upon. Depending on the intended task, additional software either in the form of a script or for more advanced uses, full-blown applications are needed. In both cases, they are often specific to the task and need to be written. Getting such software in the BeagleBone is usually pretty straightforward.

> The BeagleBone is a fully fledged computer. For many software tasks, the exact same procedure used on a desktop can be used on the BeagleBone. The notable exception is the software that requires extensive resources to be built in a practical amount of time might require more advanced techniques, such as cross compilation.

The typical process is as follows; the specifics will vary as per the projects:

1. Log in to the BeagleBone using ssh. The shipped system software does not use a password for root by default. However, some images, such as early versions of Debian, might require a specific username and/or password. Refer to the documentation for the image for the password and/or username to be used.

2. Using an editor of your choice, create the scripts or C/C++ program files. Alternatively, create the files on the desktop/laptop and copy the contents over using scp.

Standard software tools, such as make and gcc, are available natively on the BeagleBone. Depending on the distribution, you may have to install them explicitly. Details of the installation process details, such as the name of the packages and commands, will vary depending on the distribution.

3. If necessary, compile the C/C++ program on the BeagleBone.

4. Debug and repeat.

Many software packages can be built using this method. Simply copy over the source files and run, make, or configure as you would on a desktop system. The exact steps will vary between packages and should be a part of the source code or package documentation. Note that many software packages have dependencies that have to be met either by installing a distribution-provided version or building them yourself. Depending on the package, this can be a simple way but might be time consuming.

Summary

In this chapter, we looked at the two common system software distributions for the BeagleBone. We also went through the basics of downloading and running a distribution. For the BBB, this process allows a BBB in an unknown state to be restored to a factory condition. Finally, we looked at an overview of installation applications in the BeagleBone.

The upcoming chapters will be much more hands on as we apply the foundation built here and go through the process of building your first project on the BeagleBone. We will build a variation of the classic first project for embedded users, an LED flasher. While you might not have chosen to install a new distribution at this time, this process can be applied to recover from most software mistakes.

The LED flasher project will be broken into two parts. In *Chapter 3, Building an LED Flasher*, we will ease into controlling the LED and end with a basic flasher. This basic flasher will be the foundation for the advanced exercises.

Building an LED Flasher

3

Now that we have a basic foundation of what's on the BeagleBone and how to install the basic system software on it, we will proceed to the basic exercises on the BeagleBone with minimal fear of corrupting the BeagleBone. We'll get our feet wet with classic introductory exercises but, first, we'll write a **Hello, World** exercise to familiarize ourselves with the basics and then build our own embedded product—an LED flasher. This will be done in small steps, each introducing a set of skills needed for the LED flasher.

In this chapter, we will cover the following topics:

- Use a simple editor on the BeagleBone itself
- File permissions (what they are and how to determine them numerically)
- Set and examine file permissions
- Use sysfs to control the LEDs
- Read and write files using the shell language
- Loop and create delays in the shell language
- Debug shell scripts
- Flash LEDs

Setting up a foundation for the exercises

Let's go through a few basics for all the exercises in this book. The exercises in this book should work with the BeagleBone powered by the USB interface for the majority of users. However, a minority of users might have a desktop/laptop not permitting enough power to be drawn from the USB port. In this case, you will need the barrel power adapter as described in *Chapter 1, Introducing the Beagle Boards*.

All the exercises in this book assume that you will interact with the BeagleBone over the USB interface. To do this, you will need an SSH client suitable for your laptop/desktop. Refer to *Chapter 1, Introducing the Beagle Boards*, for examples of SSH clients on Linux and Windows. To recap the basics, the process is as follows:

1. Plug in the USB port and allow the BeagleBone to boot up.

2. Start the SSH client.

3. Connect to `192.168.7.2` using the SSH client.

4. Log in as `root`.

After a successful login, you will be at a shell prompt similar to this:

```
foo $
$
#
```

The exact prompt will depend on the distribution's default configuration. For the rest of the book, the prompt will be simplified to $.

> Nothing prevents the exercises from being completed on the diagnostic serial port. However, to do so, you will require the serial cable on the BBB and a terminal program. Performing the exercises with the USB interface is more straightforward for beginners without learning additional tools.

Selecting an editor

All the exercises will involve typing short pieces of text. To keep things simple, the exercises will be done using the shell script. This was chosen due to its simplicity and almost universal availability in all the common distributions on the BeagleBone. Almost all the alternative programming languages can perform the functions that are equivalent to what shell scripting performs. This makes it an ideal learning language. The ubiquity of shell scripting is the reason why many portable pieces of the setup code are written in shell scripting.

> Shell script is a language that is used to program Linux systems. It provides you with an access to the most basic system controls through a series of commands listed in a text format. The commands used in a shell script are the same commands as typed in the normal shell. In order to do the exercises, you will need to use an editor. For Linux users, they are similar to the editors that are available on the desktop/laptop.

Most distributions will offer one of the following editors:

- **vi/vim**: This is the classic Linux text editor. It is very versatile, but also one of the most cryptic editors available. For users interested in this editor, you can refer to one of the many books on vi. No other specific mention of this editor will be made in this book. If you are already familiar with this editor, feel free to use it.

- **nano/pico**: These are relatively simple editors. For Windows users, this is not too different from the basic command-line editor, edit. For beginners, this can be a good choice to get started.

Quick start with nano/pico

A simple editor to start with is the nano/pico editor. A few quickstart hints for nano/pico are as follows:

- To create or edit a file, provide the filename as the argument, as shown in the following command:

```
$ nano hello.sh
```

- This will create a file named hello.sh and open it for editing if the file does not exist. If the file already exists, it will just open the file for editing.

- Once in the editor, you can type normally.

- To exit the editor, press *Ctrl* + *X*, that is, hold down the *Ctrl* key, and then press the *X* key. If the file has been modified, you will be prompted to save or discard the changes.

More advanced topics such as search and replace are outside the scope of this book. Additional information can be found using a search engine. For the exercises in this book, these advanced features will offer minimal help.

Permissions

Linux has the concept of permissions for files. For our purposes, the main concern is the execute permission. On a desktop/laptop system with multiple users, permissions allows you to have selective access between different users. However, for an embedded system such as the BeagleBone, permissions can provide security to isolate problems either due to programmer- or user-errors. Other embedded uses of permissions are to implement an access policy for the device itself. Linux permissions come in three basic forms, namely, read, write, and execute. The meaning differs slightly between files and directories.

For our purpose, we are mainly concerned with the permission on files. Let's take a look at these permissions in detail:

- **Read**: This permission allows a file to be read and is designated by the letter r.

- **Write**: This permission allows the file to be modified and is designated by the letter w.

- **Execute**: This permission allows a file to be executed (that is, run as a program). This is the most important permission for the purpose of these exercises. Without the execute permission, the short programs we write will not run. This is designated by the letter x.

Determining the current permission

To determine the current permission of a file, use the ls command with the -l (long list) option as follows:

```
$ ls -l hello.sh
-rw-rw-r-- 1 root users 0 Aug  3 22:25 hello.sh
```

In the preceding example, the ls command is used to examine the permissions on the hello.sh file. The output of the ls command has several fields separated by spaces. The first field of text, in this case -rw-rw-r--, is the permission for the hello.sh file. For our purposes, this is the main field of concern.

> The full list of fields in the order shown is permissions, reference count, owner of the file, group owner of the file, size of the file, date of the last modification, and the name of the file.

Meaning of the permissions field

Due to Linux originating from the desktop and multiuser world, permissions can be applied to three basic groups of entities. The three groups of entities are in the order presented as follows:

- **User or owner of the file**: The owner of the file is the user, as shown in the third field of the preceding example, where root is the owner of the file.

- **Group owner of the file**: Each user in Linux is associated with a default group. When a file is created, the file has a group owner determined by the default group of the user that created it. The group owner is shown in the fourth field. In the preceding example, the group owner is users.

On a desktop system, the group can be a collection of different users with the same level of shared access. For example, on a desktop system, file access can be restricted to a group composed of all the managers in a company.

- **Other owner of the file**: Everyone else other than the user or group is the other owner of the file.

The following diagram shows the Linux permission entities relationship in a graphical form. The permissions are applied based on the most specific member.

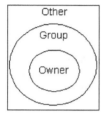

Each entity's permission is shown as a set of three characters in the order of read, write, and execute (rwx).

In the preceding example, the permissions are shown in the order listed earlier (-rw-rw-r---). Let's go through it in logical groups:

- The first character (-) is used to indicate a special file, for example, a directory d can be designed. For the purpose of the exercises, we can ignore this field.

 For more details, consult the man page for the ls command. This can be found by running man ls on a system with the man pages installed. By default, the man pages are not installed on most BeagleBone distributions. However, they are often installed on a desktop or laptop Linux system. Man pages can also be found on the Internet using a search engine.

- The next three characters (rw-) are the permissions for the owner of the file. In this case, it is for the root user. The presence of a letter means that permission is granted. If there is a - where the letter is normally present, the permission is denied; rw- here means the user has read and write permissions, but no execute permission as the last character of the group is -.

- The next three characters (rw-) are the permissions for the group owner of the file. In this case, these are the permissions for the members of the group name users. The rw- variable means anyone who is a member of the group users, but is not the user (root) who has permissions to read and write to the file, but not execute it.

- The last group of three characters (r--) are the permissions for anyone else who is not the owner of the file and is not a member of the group owner of the file. In this example, anyone is allowed to read the file, but not modify or execute it.

- The last character (-) has a special advanced meaning that can be ignored for most basic uses.

 An example of using these permissions on an embedded device, such as the BeagleBone, is building a device with a web server connected to the Internet. Permissions can be used to limit access to what can be seen using the web server.

Now that we know the basics of permissions, there is one more detail we need to be concerned with the BeagleBone, an embedded device. Embedded devices tend to have limited storage and the BeagleBone is no exception. On a desktop system with plentiful storage, permissions can be referred to symbolically just like the output of the ls command. In order to minimize the storage used by the system, many distributions on the BeagleBone require permissions to be described numerically.

Converting permissions to the numeric form

Permissions can be converted to the numeric form by following a few basic rules:

- Numeric description does not need to include the special file indication. This is the first character in the output of ls.

- Permissions for each entity are described by a separate single digit in the order of owner, group, and other. In other words, each group of rwx is represented by a single digit.

- To determine the numeric value, add each type of permission granted where:
    - Read permission has a value of 4
    - Write permission has a value of 2
    - Execute permission has a value of 1

Again, referring to the earlier example with the permissions shown as `-rw-rw-r---`, the first - character is ignored. The first entity, the owner of the file, has permissions of `rw-`. The user has read and write permissions, but not the execute permission. We add 4 and 2 (values of read and write respectively) to arrive at a total of 6. Similarly, the group owner of the file has permissions of `rw-`. Again, add 4 and 2 that gives a total of 6. For everyone else, the permission is `r--`, or only read. This gives a value of 4. Putting it all together, the numeric description of the permissions is 664.

To grant permission to an entity that does not currently have the permission, add the value of this permission. To revoke the permission for the entity, subtract the value of this permission. As an added check, the permission value should always be a value between 0 and 7 inclusive.

> Permissions are actually octal numbers. The permissions themselves are determined by a set of three bits in binary. Each octal digit represents three bits.

Setting up permissions

To change or set permissions on a file, use the Linux `chmod` command. The `chmod` command takes two parameters, namely, permissions and the name of the file to apply the permissions to.

> For readers who might have learned permissions on a desktop system where the permissions can be described symbolically, depending on the particular distribution, this might not work.

A method that works on all distributions, including desktop systems, is to describe permissions numerically. In the earlier example, we looked at the `hello.sh` file. This is going to be our first program and we will run it. Unfortunately, there are no execute permissions for the program. Let's fix it as follows:

```
$ ls -l hello.sh
-rw-rw-r-- 1 ds2 ds2 0 Aug  4 00:06 hello.sh
$ chmod 775 hello.sh
$ ls -l hello.sh
-rwxrwxr-x 1 ds2 ds2 0 Aug  4 00:06 hello.sh
```

Here, we run `chmod 775 hello.sh` to set permissions on the `hello.sh` file. Before the change, the permissions were `rw-rw-r--` (looking at just the owner/group/other part). Numerically, this is `664`. We will now add the execute permission. As per the *Converting permissions to the numeric form* section, this means we have to add `1` to each digit, which gives us the `775` permission. Running `ls -l` again confirms that the change made has the intended effect.

Exercise format and notes

Now that we have the ability to create files and an understanding of permissions, it is time to start the exercises. In the sample programs, the text will have a line number at the beginning so that they can be referred to in the text. Do not type the number and the colon used to separate them. Unless explicitly noted, there is no initial space in each line.

 Do not execute any `cd` (change directories) commands when following the exercises. The exercises are written with certain assumptions depending on which directory you are on. If you have already executed any `cd` commands beforehand, run `cd` without any parameters to set the current directory to the default home directory, as follows:

```
$ cd
```

Hello, World for the BeagleBone

Hello, World is the classic first program. While it is very simple, it will go through running programs on the BeagleBone to familiarize ourselves with the process before diving fully into LED blinking. The goal of a Hello, World program is to print this message on the screen.

Exercise 1 – creating a Hello, World program

For this exercise, we will first log in to the BeagleBone and create a file containing the Hello, World program.

We will use shell as our programming language. All the following exercises in this and the next chapter will be in shell. This language was intentionally selected to make it easy to build your own software later on without it being overly complex. The exact version of the shell will vary depending on the distribution used. However, exercises should work on all known versions. A common version of the shell with many extensions, which we will not use in the exercises, is bash. Some distributions will use a simpler and smaller shell called dash, which has fewer extensions.

Then, we will set up the permissions on the file (this step is often overlooked!), run the program, and have it print Hello, World.

To do this, follow these steps:

1. Log in to your BeagleBone. In future exercises, this step is implied and will not be explicitly called out.

2. From the shell prompt, create a text file named `hello.sh` with the following content. We go through it line by line in a bit. So, do not be too concerned if it doesn't have any meaning at this time. Do not type the line number and colon; they are there so we can refer to each line:

```
hello.sh
1: #!/bin/sh
2: # This is a Hello, World Program. The next line is blank.
3:
4: echo Hello, World
```

Let's go through this short program:

- Line 1 is a magic sequence that tells the Linux kernel this is a shell script. This must be the first line. The first two characters (#!) are a signal to the kernel that the rest of the line is the path to the interpreter for this program. In this case, the interpreter is /bin/sh, which is the basic shell.

Another example of this magic sequence is as follows:

`#!/usr/bin/python`

This is to tell the kernel that the file is a Python script and should be handed to the Python interpreter located at /usr/bin/python. The #! sequence is known as the hashbang or shebang. For more information, visit http://en.wikipedia.org/wiki/Shebang_%28Unix%29.

For most scripting languages, this first line is human readable to determine the rest of the file.

- The next line is the first line that the shell will process. In the shell, anything after the # character until the end of the line is considered a comment. The shell does nothing with the comments. They are there for the user to annotate the code. It is useful for other things, such as keeping short notes or explanations on some special code. Here, we are using the comment to indicate that the following line is blank to avoid any confusion for the people typing in the program. Comments can also be used to temporarily disable the code when debugging a program. We will try this technique later on.

- Line 3 is blank, but it points to an important part of shell programming. Blank lines do not do anything in a shell script. However, they are very useful in making the shell script easily readable. Blank lines can be used to separate logical blocks of code to provide a natural break to anyone reading it.

- Line 4 is the heart of the program. In a shell script, the echo command prints all of its parameters. In this case, we are printing Hello, World.

Now that we have a basic understanding of what this little program does, let's try to run it. To run a simple text-based program such as this shell script, we type its name in the command line as follows:

```
$ ./hello.sh
bash: ./hello.sh: Permission denied.
```

We begin the name of the program with the sequence ./, which explicitly instructs the kernel to run the program in the current directory. By default, many distributions do not have the current directory in the list of places and it will look for programs for security reasons. Imagine that you developed a device using the BeagleBone that will let people upload their own programs over the Internet to your BeagleBone. One day, while debugging, you accidently change the directory where programs are uploaded, that is, you mean to enter ls -l to look around, but as a typo, you typed sl -l. A clever user of your device might have uploaded a program called sl to do unintended evil things. If, by default, you had things configured to look in your current directory for programs to run, you might have run the uploaded program without realizing it! Despite this caution, some distributions do default to look in your current directory automatically.

The output does not look like our goal of printing Hello, World. Let's look at what went wrong. The output gives us a hint with the Permission denied message. Let's begin by examining the permissions on the file:

```
$ ls -l hello.sh

-rw-rw-r-- 1 root users 23 Aug  4 00:41 hello.sh
```

As mentioned in the earlier section, the execute permission is needed for Linux to recognize things as a program. You can see that the file lacks this permission. Let's fix this. Make the file executable using chmod, as follows:

```
$ chmod 777 hello.sh
```

Here, we are being very generous with permissions. This is a first exercise and we do not want permissions to cause problems. To review, this command gives all the permissions to anyone (the owner, members of the group, and anyone else). The permissions we are giving are read, write, and execute.

The absolute minimum permissions that are needed for a shell script to work are the read and execute permissions.

Once again, attempt to run the program:

```
$ ./hello.sh
Hello, World
```

Congratulations! You have written and executed your first program on the BeagleBone!

Let's review what you've learned:

- We built a foundation by learning how to create a file on the BeagleBone using an editor
- We looked at the concepts of permissions on Linux, learned how to check the current permissions on a file, and how to change them
- We learned that the execute permission is important in making the program runnable by Linux

Flashing the LEDs

Hello, World might be a good first exercise on the BeagleBone to build a foundation, but it doesn't leverage any of the unique embedded features of the BeagleBone. The BeagleBone can interact with the real world. Our next exercise will be a classic first exercise for embedded devices such as the BeagleBone. We will attempt to blink some of the LEDs on the BeagleBone over the course of the next few exercises.

LEDs on the BeagleBone

The BeagleBone boards come with four programmable LEDs. These are the same LEDs that are used to indicate the software flashing status located next to the RJ45 Ethernet connector. On the BBW, the LEDs are green, whereas on the BBB, the LEDs are blue. The LEDs can be programmed in the same way on both the BBB and BBW. They are the LEDs that we will be blinking in our exercises.

You can see all the four LEDs on the BeagleBone White and BeagleBone Black turned on in the following image:

Exercise 2 – taking control of the LEDs

The goal of this exercise is to take control of the LEDs on the BeagleBone and turn them on. By default, on most distributions, the LEDs are configured to blink the status of the system. We will disable the blinking of the LEDs that shows the system status. For now, we will turn on the LED to check whether we have control. In the next exercise, we will add the additional code to turn off and blink the LEDs.

> As the LEDs on the BBW and BBB are of different colors, some versions of software at the time of writing this book might refer to the LEDs on the BBB as green or vice versa. This is a minor cosmetic simplification in the system software, as the internal hardware between the BBB and BBW is very similar.

Figuring out the LED controls

Since the Linux software for the BeagleBone is constantly being updated, the first step is to determine the name used on your BeagleBone for the LEDs. The LEDs are controlled by a set of special files. Writing to the special file allows the LED to be turned on and off or configured for other things.

These special files are the `sysfs` files. The `sysfs` file allows you to control many aspects of the Linux system by reading or writing to the appropriate file. For more details, search for `sysfs` on a search engine.

The special files to control the LEDs are located in the subdirectories under
/sys/class/leds. Their contents can be examined with the ls command.

Earlier, we looked at using ls -1 to provide us with details such as the permissions.
Running ls without the -1 command allows you to take a quick look at which files
are available in a directory, as shown here:

```
$ ls /sys/class/leds
beaglebone:green:usr0   beaglebone:green:usr2
beaglebone:green:usr1   beaglebone:green:usr3
```

In most systems, there will be four entries here. There can be additional entries,
if expansion boards are installed. The entries that are of interest to us are the ones
beginning with beaglebone as the name. Usually, there will only be four entries
containing beaglebone. Each entry corresponds to one LED. The last part of each
entry, usrN where N is a number from 0 to 3, refers to the correspondingly named
LED in the manual. If your BeagleBone shows slightly different names, replace
them with the corresponding name in your version of the exercise. For example, a
future version of the software might have entries named beaglebone:blue:usr0,
beaglebone:blue:usr1, and so on to reflect the BBB having blue LEDs.

Each entry listed is a directory containing the set of special files that allows us to
configure and control the LEDs. With the names of the LEDs noted, let's examine
the controls available:

```
$ ls /sys/class/leds/beaglebone:green:usr2
brightness   device   max_brightness   power   subsystem   trigger   uevent
```

These are the special files associated with the usr2 LED. The files that are of interest
to us are brightness and trigger. We will look at each one as we use them.

Disconnecting the LEDs temporarily from the system

By default, on most distributions, the LEDs are set up to blink the system status.
LEDs on Linux can be attached to show different activities, such as how busy the
system is, the network activity, or when something is written to the flash memory.
Linux refers to them as triggers. Triggers are configured by the trigger special file.
To disconnect an LED's trigger, we can set the trigger to none. A trigger can be set
by writing none to the trigger file.

To see what triggers are available, use the `cat` command to read the `trigger` file, for example:

```
$ cat /sys/class/leds/beaglebone:green:usr2/trigger
none nand-disk mmc0 timer oneshot [heartbeat] backlight
gpio cpu0 default-on transient
```

The currently configured trigger is shown in brackets. In the preceding example, `heartbeat`, is currently configured. The `cat` command is not limited to special files and it can be used to read any file.

In a shell script, a file can be written using the greater than character (>). The character causes what is normally seen on the screen to be written in the file. This is known as redirection or redirecting a command to a file. Earlier in the Hello, World exercise, we used the `echo` command to print a message. The `echo` command combined with redirection allows us to write to a file in a shell script.

You can restore the system LED behavior by simply rebooting. These changes are not permanent.

Turning on an LED

After disconnecting the LED from the preconfigured system uses, the LEDs can be used for other purposes, such as our LED blinking exercise. Like the triggers, the LED states are controlled by a special file. Turning on an LED is accomplished by writing to the `brightness` file. Writing a `0` to the file turns off the LED, whereas writing a nonzero value to the LED turns it on. For our exercise, we will use the value `255`.

LEDs on Linux can be potentially dimmed. This can be done by having Linux's send commands to dedicated hardware or by the Linux kernel toggling an LED rapidly for a specific period of time. The latter technique is known as **pulse width modulation (PWM)**. By default, dimming is not enabled on the BeagleBone. A large value, such as `255`, is purposely chosen so the readers using other future Linux distributions can choose to preconfigure dimming or brightness and won't be confused by a dimly lit LED. It should be noted that all the LEDs use the same interface. Only the Linux kernel needs to be reconfigured to change between different hardware.

The current state of the LED can be examined by reading the `brightness` special file. This can be done using the `cat` command as follows:

```
$ cat /sys/class/leds/beaglebone:green:usr2/brightness
0
```

Using the controls in a program

Now that we know how to disconnect the LEDs from the system control and turn them on, let's put it together in a program.

Type the following program and name it `ledon.sh`:

```
ledon.sh
1: #!/bin/sh
2: # Replace the names with what is used on your system
3: # Disconnect all 4 LEDs on the BeagleBone so we can use it.
4: echo none > /sys/class/leds/beaglebone:green:usr0/trigger
5: echo none > /sys/class/leds/beaglebone:green:usr1/trigger
6: echo none > /sys/class/leds/beaglebone:green:usr2/trigger
7: echo none > /sys/class/leds/beaglebone:green:usr3/trigger
8: # Turn on all 4 LEDs
9: echo 255 > /sys/class/leds/beaglebone:green:usr0/brightness
10: echo 255 > /sys/class/leds/beaglebone:green:usr1/brightness
11: echo 255 > /sys/class/leds/beaglebone:green:usr2/brightness
12: echo 255 > /sys/class/leds/beaglebone:green:usr3/brightness
```

Let's analyze the preceding program:

- The first line tells the Linux kernel that this is a shell script.

- From lines 3 to 7, the LEDs are disconnected from the system one by one by writing `none` to the `trigger` control file. For the users who have noted a different name earlier, replace the name used here with the one noted. The lines beginning with # are comments used to help you understand what it does.

- Lines 8 to 12 turn on each LED one by one by writing 255 to the special `brightness` file.

Be sure to set the execute permission in the `ledon.sh` file if you haven't done so. As a check, an inspection of the permissions should show something like this:

```
$ ls -l ledon.sh
-rwxrwxrwx 1 root users 617 Aug  4 02:12 ledon.sh
```

Run your program by typing the following command:

```
$ ./ledon.sh
```

There is no output on your SSH session. This entire program only changes the LEDs. If all four LEDs turn on and remain on, congratulations!

Exercise 3 – simple blinking

In order to write a program to blink an LED, we need to do a few things. From a programming standpoint, the following needs to be done:

1. Turn on the LED.
2. Wait for some time.
3. Turn off the LED.
4. Wait for some time.
5. Finally, repeat step 1.

From the *Exercise 2 – taking control of the LEDs* section, we have learned how to do the first part of the LED blinker. In this exercise, we will learn how to do the rest and complete our LED blinker. Since this book is about learning to use the BeagleBone, we will focus only on the aspects of shell programming needed to complete this exercise.

Delays in the program

One useful characteristic of Linux is that it is a multitasking operating system. What this means is that Linux will allow multiple programs to run simultaneously. This is accomplished by letting each program run for a little bit, and then switching to another program. When a program is waiting for time to pass, the right thing for it to do is to let Linux know; so, it can let other programs run. In shell scripting, this can be done with the sleep command. The sleep command takes the number of seconds to wait before continuing.

 In addition to yielding to other programs running, the sleep command allows the Linux kernel to reduce power consumption if there are no other programs to run. This can be important in an embedded system running from a limited power source, such as a battery.

Repeating things with loops

Until now, we have repeated things by retyping and modifying text as needed. Shell scripting can repeat things in a controlled fashion. This is known as looping. For this exercise, we will create a loop that repeats until it is stopped. This is known as an infinite loop.

 For many types of programming, infinite loops can be a bug. However, for many embedded applications, it is often desirable for one program to always remain running. For example, we are creating an embedded device that blinks an LED. A common expectation is that it will continue to blink nonstop.

In this exercise, we will use a `while` loop. Other loops are available, but will not be discussed in this book. A `while` loop will continue to loop as long as the test condition is `true`. By using a constant `true` as the test condition, it becomes an infinite loop. Here is a fragment of code illustrating such a loop:

```
while :
do
        # Code to repeat
done
```

There are a few new concepts to note here:

- In a shell script, the test condition for a `while` loop is provided after the `while` keyword. For this example, the test condition is `:`. A `:` sign is a do nothing operation that always returns `true`. For readers familiar with other programming languages such as C, this is equivalent to a `while(1)` loop.

- Unlike other shell commands seen so far, the `while` loop consists of multiple lines. The loop begins with the `while` keyword along with the test condition. The part of the program to loop, known as a block, is delineated by the pair of keywords, namely, `do` and `done`. Everything between the `do` and `done` keywords will be repeated.

- The block of repeated code is indented. Earlier, we mentioned that spaces are ignored in a shell script, but they are useful for readability of the code. Shell scripting does not require indentation. By indenting the repeated block, one can quickly deduce which code is being repeated without having to look at it line by line.

Turning off an LED

In the *Exercise 2 – taking control of the LEDs* section, we mentioned turning off an LED. Similar to turning on an LED, turning off an LED is done by merely writing a 0 to the brightness special file. While this is not a new concept, turning off an LED is merely setting the brightness to 0.

Blinking the LEDs

Now that we have all the basic elements needed for this exercise, let's put it into action with a program. Enter the following program and name it ledblink.sh:

```
ledblink.sh
1: #!/bin/sh
2: # Blink the 4 LEDs
3: # Run the following code forever
4: while :
5: do
6:     # Turn on the 4 LEDs
7:     echo 255 > /sys/class/leds/beaglebone:green:usr0/brightness
10:    echo 255 > /sys/class/leds/beaglebone:green:usr1/brightness
11:    echo 255 > /sys/class/leds/beaglebone:green:usr2/brightness
12:    echo 255 > /sys/class/leds/beaglebone:green:usr3/brightness
13:    # sleep 1
14:    echo 0 > /sys/class/leds/beaglebone:green:usr0/brightness
15:    echo 0 > /sys/class/leds/beaglebone:green:usr1/brightness
16:    echo 0 > /sys/class/leds/beaglebone:green:usr2/brightness
17:    echo 0 > /sys/class/leds/beaglebone:green:usr3/brightness
18:    # sleep 1
19: done
```

Make sure to set the executable permission in ledblink.sh if you have not done so.

 If you jumped ahead and ran the program, it will appear to be stuck. The prompt never returns. To break out of this, press *Ctrl + C*. You might need to press it multiple times.

Before running it, let's go through the program:

- Lines 1 to 3 are the usual shell program lines that tells the system that this is a shell, and then leaves comments to the users of the program.

- Line 4 starts with a while loop. The contents to loop are designated by the block delimiters beginning with line 5 and ending with line 19.

- Lines 6 to 18 are the lines to repeat. They turn on the LED as described, pause, turn off the LED, pause again, and then repeat the entire cycle again.

Run the program using the following command:

```
$ ./ledblink.sh
```

Looking at the LEDs

Due to an error introduced purposely for this exercise, the LEDs do not seem to be blinking by the normal definition of blink. Let's debug our program.

The first thing you might notice is that this program does not immediately return to the prompt. This program has an infinite loop that continues until stopped. To stop it, you need to press *Ctrl + C*. It might be necessary to press it multiple times. Stop pressing it when the command prompt appears.

Load the program in an editor and view the program. See whether you can spot the error. Visual inspection of the program is one of the methods of debugging. If nothing stands out, the next step is to review what is known. We ran the program and the LEDs appears to stay on, but they also appeared to be somewhat dimmer than what we saw in exercise 2. An astute observer might notice that the LEDs are blinking, but they are just blinking too fast!

With these clues in mind, let's review the code. The entire program repeats the lines 6 to 18. So, let's focus our attention on these lines. Lines 6 to 12 turn on the LEDs as in the previous exercise. We also know that the LED does successfully turn on even though it might appear dimmer.

The next line, 13, mentions sleep. Sleep as described before is a way of waiting. Looking at it closely, we see #. Referring back to the first part of this chapter, the # character tells the shell to ignore everything after it. So, effectively, the sleep command is ignored. Looking further at line 18, we see a similar problem. Remove the # character from lines 13 and 18 and save the file.

Run ledblink.sh as before and observe the LEDs.

If you see all four LEDs blinking in unison slowly once every second, congratulations! You have successfully blinked the LEDs on the BeagleBone.

Troubleshooting

If your LEDs did not blink slowly in unison once a second, something is wrong. Exercises 2 and 3 were designed to be run one after another. If you did them in two sessions or simply power cycled the BeagleBone, you need to rerun exercise 2. Exercise 2 reconfigures the LEDs to allow programmable control. This reconfiguration will remain as long as the BeagleBone is not rebooted. Assuming that it was completed correctly, you can repeat it by just running `ledon.sh`.

If, during any step, you see permission denied errors, verify the permissions. Although most editors will preserve permissions, it is possible for the editor to remove the execute permission. Permissions can be restored by running the following command:

```
$ chmod 777 ledblink.sh
```

Exercise 4 – advanced blinking

In the preceding exercise, we created a basic blinker. Using the same concept, we can create more advanced blinking that offers a different pattern. This exercise does not introduce any new concepts and purposely offers less hand-holding to allow you to practice the concepts. In exercise 3, all four LEDs flashed in unison. In this exercise, we will sequence the LEDs one at a time. With a little modification, the LEDs can be made to bounce back and forth in a scanning fashion. In this exercise, we will also combine the configuration from exercise 2 using the following code:

```
 myblink.sh
1: #!/bin/sh
2: # Replace the names with what is used on your system
3: # Disconnect all 4 LEDs on the BeagleBone so we can use it.
4: echo none > /sys/class/leds/beaglebone:green:usr0/trigger
5: echo none > /sys/class/leds/beaglebone:green:usr1/trigger
6: echo none > /sys/class/leds/beaglebone:green:usr2/trigger
7: echo none > /sys/class/leds/beaglebone:green:usr3/trigger
8: # Start with all 4 LEDs off
9: echo 0 > /sys/class/leds/beaglebone:green:usr0/brightness
10: echo 0 > /sys/class/leds/beaglebone:green:usr1/brightness
11: echo 0 > /sys/class/leds/beaglebone:green:usr2/brightness
12: echo 0 > /sys/class/leds/beaglebone:green:usr3/brightness
13:
14: while :
15: do
16:    echo 255 > /sys/class/leds/beaglebone:green:usr0/brightness
17:    sleep 1
18:    echo 0 > /sys/class/leds/beaglebone:green:usr0/brightness
```

```
19:    echo 255 > /sys/class/leds/beaglebone:green:usr1/brightness
20:    sleep 1
21:    echo 0 > /sys/class/leds/beaglebone:green:usr1/brightness
22:    echo 255 > /sys/class/leds/beaglebone:green:usr2/brightness
23:    sleep 1
24:    echo 0 > /sys/class/leds/beaglebone:green:usr2/brightness
25:    echo 255 > /sys/class/leds/beaglebone:green:usr3/brightness
26:    sleep 1
27:    echo 0 > /sys/class/leds/beaglebone:green:usr3/brightness
28: done
```

Remember to make this executable before you attempt to run the preceding command. A quick analysis of the program is as follows:

- Lines 3 to 12 are a variation of exercise 2. Instead of turning on the LEDs, all four LEDs are turned off for an initial state.

- By including lines 4 to 7, we ensure that the BeagleBone can run this program when powered on. In exercise 3, we rely on exercise 2 being run immediately beforehand. Including the lines 4 to 7 lifts this requirement.

- Lines 16 to 27 cycles through the LEDs one at a time. We turn on one LED and wait a second, so someone watching can see that the LED is on. Then, we immediately turn off this LED and turn on the adjacent LED. This is repeated until we get to the last LED. The last thing we do is turn off the LED, as the first thing that is done is turning on the first LED. This makes it look like the LEDs are wrapped around.

Summary

In this chapter, we went through the basic foundation to get a basic program on the BeagleBone. We looked at using a simple editor on the BeagleBone. Then, you learned about Linux file permissions. Linux file permissions are divided into three groups, namely, user, group, and other. Each group can have read, write, and execute permissions. We also looked at calculating the numeric representation of the permissions. The permissions can be examined using the ls command and set using the chmod command.

Using this basic foundation, we dived into our first Hello, World program on the BeagleBone. While being simple, it illustrated the importance of permissions. Building upon this with exercises 1 and 2, you learned about the sysfs files and how to use them to control the LEDs on the BeagleBone. We controlled the LEDs by first disconnecting them from the system control, and then turning them on and off by writing to the sysfs files using the echo command and shell redirection.

In the next few exercises, you learned how to repeat things and add delays using the shell `while` loop construct and the `sleep` command. Using the loop construct and controlled delays, we flashed the LEDs in a controllable pace. In the process of the exercises, we looked at several debugging techniques. These included using the shell # character to disable lines and stopping a loop by pressing *Ctrl* + *C*. Combining everything together, we culminated in a fancy LED blinker to blink the LED in a pattern that will work when powered up.

Building upon all of this, we will look at other aspects of programming the BeagleBone in the next chapter. Now that the core of our LED blinker is working, the next chapter is about refining the LED blinker into an embedded device by starting it as the power is turned on and giving it a user interface.

4
Refining the LED Flasher

In the previous chapter, we completed the classic introductory exercises that started the LED flasher project. Building upon those exercises, we will improve the LED flasher and turn the BeagleBone into an LED flasher project.

In this chapter, we will cover the following topics:

- The I2C bus
- Accessing the I2C devices
- Adding a user interface to our flasher
- Starting the flasher when powered on

Just as before, no additional hardware is needed; the BeagleBone board alone will suffice. The difference between the BBB and BBW will be discussed. There are slight differences between the BeagleBone boards that run Debian and Angström.

The I2C bus

A common way to connect the peripherals that do not require a very high communication speed to an embedded system is using a protocol known as I2C.

 Inter-Integrated Circuit (I2C) is a protocol originally developed by Philips Semiconductors (now NXP). I2C is also known as IIC.

I2C is a simple serial protocol that uses two signal wires. In the simplest configuration used by many setups, there is one master and one or more slave devices. For the BeagleBone, the master will be the BeagleBone and the slave devices will be peripherals. Each slave device (we will shorten to just device) is uniquely identified by a 7-bit address.

Later versions of the I2C protocol support an extended address that allows more devices on a single bus.

The serial bus, as originally defined, runs at 100 kHz; however, later revisions allowed 400 kHz and faster variations enabled all the devices on the bus to operate at the higher speed. So, a worst case speed figure is 100 kBits per second shared between all devices on the bus.

 Everything here is on a per-I2C-bus basis. There can be multiple I2C buses each with its own master. Addresses are only unique on a bus. The BeagleBone has multiple I2C buses available.

Examples of some devices that can be connected over I2C are as follows:

- Sensors such as temperature sensors, light sensors, accelerometers, magnetometers, and gyroscopes
- Small amounts of nonvolatile memory

Accessing I2C

Under Linux, many details of I2C are abstracted away from the user. For basic uses, only the bus number and the address of the device are needed. For our purposes, an I2C device can be accessed in two general ways. In an ideal world, the I2C device would be fully handled by an appropriate Linux kernel driver. This way, different hardware of the same type would appear to be the same for the userland applications, irrespective of whether the hardware is really connected by I2C. However, not all devices have drivers written for them. In addition, for debugging and experimentation, it is desirable to explicitly talk to an I2C device using the bus number and address.

In Linux, this lower-level userland interface is available for debugging and experimentation. There are a few basic sets of tools to allow simple access using the shell.

The I2C tools

The I2C tools (`http://www.lm-sensors.org/wiki/I2CTools`) are a set of utilities used to view the I2C bus on a Linux machine. The I2C tools can attempt to identify which addresses on an I2C bus contain a device and whether they are claimed by a driver. This can be useful when connecting new I2C devices. It can also attempt to read or write to a device on a very low-level basis.

To determine what devices are connected on an I2C bus, use `i2cdetect`.

 There are some uncommon devices that might not respond in a reasonable manner to the probes used by `i2cdetect`. Use this tool with caution. This is less of an issue on embedded platforms, as the expected devices on I2C are generally known ahead of time and can be cross-checked with a datasheet.

The `i2cdetect` command has the following two main uses:

- To determine the number of visible buses on a Linux system. To use it in this manner, use the `-l` option.
- To probe an I2C bus for devices on the bus. Probing for devices on an I2C bus means searching for devices on the bus by sending out a mostly harmless request on the bus and looking for responses. This can be done using `i2cdetect -r N`, where `N` is the bus number as listed by `i2cdetect`.

We will try out each of these in the following exercise. Other I2C tools for reading and writing to an I2C device include `i2cget` and `i2cset`. However, they are designed to work with devices that do not have a kernel driver configured. The stock BeagleBone configuration has proper kernel drivers for all the I2C devices on the BeagleBone.

Exercise 1

We will use the `i2cdetect` command on the BeagleBone to identify the devices on the I2C bus. As before, use SSH to connect to your BeagleBone. All commands are entered using the shell.

First, let's determine the I2C buses on the BeagleBone with the `-l` option, as shown here:

```
$ i2cdetect -l
```

```
root@beaglebone:~# i2cdetect -l
i2c-0    i2c            OMAP I2C adapter      I2C adapter
i2c-1    i2c            OMAP I2C adapter      I2C adapter
root@beaglebone:~#
```

Your output should be similar to the preceding one. This output tells us that there are two known I2C buses, namely, `bus 0` and `bus 1`. The buses use a driver that identifies itself as `OMAP I2C adapter`.

The AM335x SoC used in the BeagleBone shares many parts with the OMAP3530 and the DM3730 SoCs used in the BeagleBoards. The OMAP I2C adapter was originally named for the I2C hardware in the OMAP3530 SoC. This same I2C hardware is also present in the AM335x SoC.

If you don't see the preceding output, the most likely problems are either you don't have the I2C tools installed on your image or there was a typo. Note that the option is a lower case l not 1. An error message similar to command not found suggests that the I2C tools are not installed. At the time of writing this book, the I2C tools are part of the standard image. The rest of the I2C exercises in this chapter assume that the I2C tools are installed.

The next part of this exercise is to look at devices available on the I2C bus with the i2cdetect command. From the first part of the exercise, we know there are two buses, 0 and 1 (referred as i2c-0 and i2c-1 in the preceding example).

To look at the devices on a bus, we use the i2cdetect -r N command where N is the bus number. The -r option is needed; so i2cdetect will use a read method to probe for a device, as follows:

```
$ i2cdetect -r 0
```

Some devices might have side effects when they are read. The stock BeagleBone I2C devices behave reasonably but consult the device documentation for other devices. Also, consult the i2cdetect man page for additional details.

As probing some devices might not be safe, the following command will ask you to confirm prior to doing anything. Answer y when asked, as shown here:

```
root@beaglebone:~# i2cdetect -r 0
WARNING! This program can confuse your I2C bus, cause data loss and
worse!
I will probe file /dev/i2c-0 using read byte commands.
I will probe address range 0x03-0x77.
Continue? [Y/n] y
     0  1  2  3  4  5  6  7  8  9  a  b  c  d  e  f
00:          -- -- -- -- -- -- -- -- -- -- -- -- --
10: -- -- -- -- -- -- -- -- -- -- -- -- -- -- -- --
20: -- -- -- -- UU -- -- -- -- -- -- -- -- -- -- --
30: -- -- -- -- UU -- -- -- -- -- -- -- -- -- -- --
```

```
40: -- -- -- -- -- -- -- -- -- -- -- -- -- -- -- --
50: UU -- -- -- -- -- -- -- -- -- -- -- -- -- -- --
60: -- -- -- -- -- -- -- -- -- -- -- -- -- -- -- --
70: UU -- -- -- -- -- -- --
root@beaglebone:~#
```

If successful, you should see the preceding output. It will vary slightly between the BBB and BBW. The output is presented in a table form. Each line of the table represents 16 possible device addresses. The numbers in the row and column labels are in hexadecimal (base 16). The vertical numbers (or the row labels) are the first part of a two-digit hex number. The number in the first line of the table (or the column labels) is the second digit. To get the address of the device being referred to, add the two numbers, or to save math, just replace the zero from the first number and replace it with the second number.

The following table explains the preceding section in detail:

Value	Meaning
--	This means that there is nothing at this address.
UU	This means that something might be at the address but is currently unavailable. Most likely, the device at that address is under the control of a kernel driver. Also, drivers can claim addresses without a device.
Two hex digits	This means that a device is at the address and is available for claiming a driver.

In the preceding sample output, UU is at 0x24, 0x34, 0x50, and 0x70. This tells us that there is a driver claiming these addresses.

> Without going into too many details for an introduction, some of the interesting devices are as follows:
> - 0x24: Power Management Integrated Circuits (PMIC)
> - 0x50: EEPROM
> - 0x70: TDA998x (HDMI framer, BBB only)

As there are two I2C buses, let's look at the second bus:

```
$ i2cdetect -y -r 1
```

This is a slightly different variation in the i2cdetect command. This time, we add the -y option to skip the confirmation. The output should be similar to the following:

```
root@beaglebone:~# i2cdetect -y -r 1
     0  1  2  3  4  5  6  7  8  9  a  b  c  d  e  f
00:          -- -- -- -- -- -- -- -- -- -- -- -- --
10: -- -- -- -- -- -- -- -- -- -- -- -- -- -- -- --
20: -- -- -- -- -- -- -- -- -- -- -- -- -- -- -- --
30: -- -- -- -- -- -- -- -- -- -- -- -- -- -- -- --
40: -- -- -- -- -- -- -- -- -- -- -- -- -- -- -- --
50: -- -- -- -- UU UU UU UU -- -- -- -- -- -- -- --
60: -- -- -- -- -- -- -- -- -- -- -- -- -- -- -- --
70: -- -- -- -- -- -- -- --
root@beaglebone:~#
```

In the preceding example, we can see that there are four possible devices that are claimed or at least reserved by a kernel driver. The rest of the bus is apparently free. The four devices are at 0x54, 0x55, 0x56, and 0x57.

> In reality, these four addresses are reserved by the EEPROM driver, but there is really no hardware here. The BeagleBone expansion system, capes, requires an I2C EEPROM to allow the expansion board to be automatically configured. The kernel reserves these four addresses for the I2C EEPROM on the capes.

If your i2cdetect command generates outputs similar to the preceding one, then you have successfully completed this exercise.

The I2C devices on the BeagleBone

The BeagleBone by itself contains a few I2C devices as seen in the preceding exercise. These include the power management controller and an I2C EEPROM.

> **Electrically Erasable Programmable Read Only Memory (EEPROM)** is a type of nonvolatile memory often used to store configuration or identification information.

The PMIC generates the voltages applied to the SoC and other bits of hardware. A mistake in programming this device can cause permanent damage to the BeagleBone. We will avoid this device in our exercises.

The I2C EEPROM on the BeagleBone is used to identify the board to the software. This EEPROM can be written into but there are many safeguards in place to prevent corruption of the contents. A corrupt EEPROM can be repaired with software. This is the device we will use for our exercises.

Exercise 2

In this exercise, we will read the identification EEPROM on the BeagleBone and display it. From the preceding exercise, we know that the EEPROM is at the address 0x50 on the bus 0. We also know that a kernel driver has claimed the device. This was seen when we ran i2cdetect on the bus 0 and saw UU on the line labeled 50 under the column labeled 0.

There is a Linux kernel driver for standard I2C EEPROM devices. In this exercise, we'll read the I2C EEPROM using the kernel driver. The kernel driver presents the EEPROM as a special file. In order to read the content, we will need to use a new shell command, dd. The dd command is similar to the cat command introduced previously, and it will allow us to specify portions of the file to read. The options to dd that we are interested in are shown in the following table:

The dd parameter	Meaning
if=NAME	This tells dd to read from the file called NAME
bs=N	This sets the size of chunks dd will read at a time
count=N	This tells dd the number of chunks to read
skip=N	This tells dd the number of chunks to skip before reading

With these options, we can read only the bytes in the EEPROM of interest. The BeagleBone EEPROM contains binary data, and we need to be specific to avoid dealing with binary data that might not be printable.

Like the **LED** special files used in *Chapter 3, Building an LED Flasher*, the EEPROM is presented in another special file. For EEPROM, the file is at /sys/bus/i2c/devices/0-0050/eeprom.

The /sys/bus/i2c/devices directory contains all the known I2C devices on the system. The 0-0050 parameter refers to the bus 0 and address 0x50. The file eeprom is the way through which the kernel EEPROM driver presents the data.

The EEPROM data format is in the BeagleBone software reference manual available at http://www.beagleboard.org/Support/Hardware%20Support.

For our purpose, the 8 bytes located at the offset 4 from the beginning are of interest. This contains a string that will identify the flavor of the BeagleBone.

 This string originated in the bigger development boards for the SoC used in the BeagleBone. It is used by the system software to identify the board type.

Putting it all together, we get the following command:

```
$ dd if=/sys/bus/i2c/devices/0-0050/eeprom bs=1 skip=4 count=8
```

The following table explains every part of the preceding command:

The dd parameter	Meaning
if=/sys/bus/i2c/ devices/0-0050/eeprom	This tells dd the file to read from
bs=1	This sets the chunk size into 1-byte chunks
skip=4	This tells skip to offset 4; skip takes the number of blocks to skip but we have set the block size to 1 byte, so we skip 4 bytes
count=8	This reads 8 bytes

The output of the preceding command is as follows:

```
root@beaglebone:~# dd if=/sys/bus/i2c/devices/0-0050/eeprom bs=1 skip=4
count=8
A335BNLT8+0 records in
8+0 records out
8 bytes (8 B) copied, 0.0101364 s, 0.8 kB/s
root@beaglebone:~#
```

Note the output of the command, A335BNLT, runs right into the summary from dd. As described earlier, the content of the EEPROM is binary data. The dd command will display exactly what is read. As the data is binary, the EEPROM does not include things such as a new line to break up the data from the summary from dd. In the later exercises, we will save the output of dd to a file to separate the summary from dd and the actual data.

The output of this command will obviously differ between the BBB and BBW. The preceding example was done on a BBB and the output is A335BNLT. For the BBW, the string will be A335BONE.

If your output is similar to the preceding one, you have successfully completed the exercise!

Now that we have gotten our feet wet with I2C, let's go back to the LED flasher we started building in *Chapter 3, Building an LED Flasher*. When we left the LED flasher, the LED flasher required us to log in and manually start it. The only way to change the flash behavior is to change the program.

User interfaces

Until this point, the LED flasher has hardcoded parameters. It would be very nice to control the flashing with a user interface. The BeagleBone is naturally connected to the network. So far, all our accesses have been via a network over the USB interface. The BeagleBone also has an Ethernet interface that we have not used yet. Our next few exercises are to add an interface to change the behavior of the LED flasher.

 Up to this point, all our exercises were done using shell scripting. The BeagleBone ships with another language, BoneScript, which allows the BeagleBone to be programmed using a language similar to JavaScript. Shell script was chosen for exercises over BoneScript to provide an easier path for programmers who are not web oriented to transition to the BeagleBone environment.

Design

Our user interface will be accessed through a web browser. The web pages will be served using the same web server shipped with the BeagleBone that BoneScript uses. Communications between the LED flasher software and the browser will be done through a very simple BoneScript page. The following flowchart explains the process in detail:

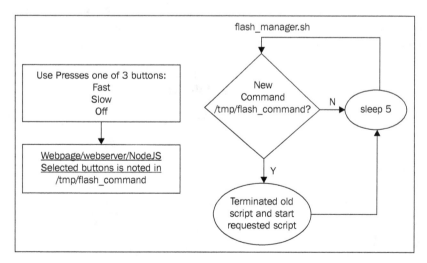

The user interface will offer three different settings, namely, a slow flash, a fast flash, and no flash. We will take a simplistic approach to support the three modes by dividing the tasks into the following four pieces:

- A shell script that just blanks the LED to implement the no flash option.

- A shell script that implements a slow flash.

- A shell script that implements a fast flash.

- A manager script that watches for input from the UI. Its job is to stop and start the preceding scripts based on the UI input.

The first three scripts are the same as what we wrote in the previous chapter with a few minor modifications to integrate with the manager script.

As shipped, the BeagleBone software starts a web server built on top of Nodejs. Nodejs (http://nodejs.org/) is another language but, for our exercises, we will only use it in a limited fashion in the form of BoneScript to provide a web-based user interface.

 The exercises intentionally ignore security issues in order to keep them manageable. While the same concepts are reusable in your own project, anything that is somewhat open should also be designed with security in mind.

Exercise 3

In this exercise, we will serve a custom page using the web server that is shipped with the BeagleBone. The BeagleBone ships with a web server that contains a few basic support pages. We will add our own page and verify that it works. The location for the web page will differ slightly depending on the system software on the BeagleBone. Debian users will have one location and Angström users will have another location.

From a shell, create a file on the web page at the location for your software. The specifications for different users are as follows:

- For Angström users (/usr/share/bone101), use the following command:

  ```
  $ pico /usr/share/bone101/hello.html
  ```

- For Debian users (/var/lib/cloud9), use the following command:

  ```
  $ pico /var/lib/cloud9/hello.html
  ```

Replace pico with your editor of choice. Type and save the following text (once again, do not type the line numbers):

```
1:<title>Hello, World</title>
2:<h1>Hello, World</h1>
```

This is a simple HTML file that we will serve. For the readers who are not familiar with HTML, line 1 sets the title of the page to Hello, World and line 2 puts Hello, World in a large heading 1 size text in the main page.

To test our web page, we need to start a web browser. This page and other web pages that we created use only the basic features and work with most web browsers, such as Firefox. Before trying to load our page, let's verify our setup.

Let's refer back to how you logged in to the BeagleBone with SSH; you entered an IP address: 192.168.7.2. If you used a different address, replace this address in http://192.168.7.2/. Open a web browser on your laptop/desktop. Tell your browser to go to a URL. Usually, this can be done by clicking on the address bar, by pressing *Ctrl + L*, or by selecting **Open URL** from the **File** menu and pressing *Enter*.

If you are successful, the following page will appear. This is the default web page on the BeagleBone. It redirects to the support page.

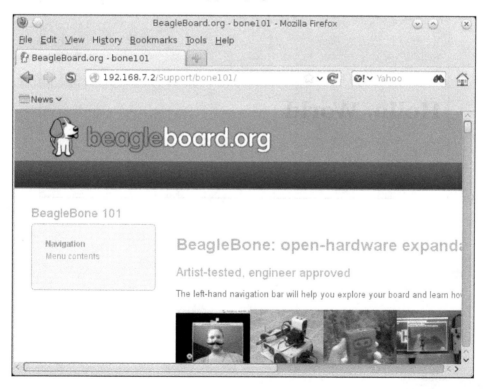

Troubleshooting

For the readers who don't see the preceding web page, the troubleshooting steps will depend on what does appear. If you see an error about server not found or server not responding, double-check the URL. It should consist of the `http://` text followed by the IP address and then end with / (slash). If the error persists after verifying the URL, check for any filtering, blocking, or firewall software on your laptop/desktop.

If you see an **Error 404** message, double check the URL. Pay attention to any extra text at the end. While unlikely, there is a possibility that the software on your BeagleBone is corrupted. After verifying that the URL is typed correctly and there are no problems on the laptop/desktop, consider reinstalling the system software on your BeagleBone. The process is described in *Chapter 2, Software in the BeagleBone*.

Loading your first web page

Once you have successfully loaded the default web page, you can move on to loading your first BeagleBone web page. Go to the browser and enter `http://192.168.7.2/hello.html`. The following page will appear:

Troubleshooting the BeagleBone web server access

If you see an **Error 404** message, check whether you have used the correct location for your system software. The location to place the web page differs for Angström and Debian. The locations provided are correct at the time of writing this book. If the location appears to be correct, verify the permission on the file, as follows (it should be universally readable):

```
root@beaglebone:/usr/share/bone101# ls -l
/usr/share/bone101/hello.html
-rw-r--r-- 1 root root 50 Jan  1 00:10 /usr/share/bone101/hello.html
root@beaglebone:/usr/share/bone101#
```

If the permissions differ, use chmod to change the permissions, as follows:

```
$ chmod 644 /usr/share/bone101/hello.html
```

Now that you have loaded your first web page, note the place where you created the hello.html file. We will use this information in a later exercise to place the file for our user interface.

Exercise 4

Now that we have successfully created our own web page and served it using the BeagleBone's web server, we will work on creating the backend first. In this exercise, we will create the manager shell script.

Shell variables

Like any other programming language, shell scripts have variables. Variables are a way of saving information so that it can be used later. A shell variable can save the output from another shell command, or it can be assigned data from a file. Another use for a shell variable is to save the state information.

In a shell script, a variable name can consist of letters, numbers, and a few selected symbols. Variable names are case sensitive. For example, Counter and COUNTER are two different variables. For simplicity, we will use all capital letters in our variable names.

Shell variables can be directly assigned values using the = operator, for example:

```
COUNTER=2
```

This sets the shell variable COUNTER to a value of 2. Shell variables can also be assigned the data from a file with the read command, as follows:

```
read VARIABLE < FILENAME
```

There are two new concepts here, which are as follows:

- The shell command read is used to take input from the terminal and save the output to VARIABLE.

- The < character is another form of redirection as introduced in *Chapter 3, Building an LED Flasher*. Here, the < character tells the shell to read from a file and use that data as if it was typed. This is the complement of >, which places the output of a command into a file.

Unlike other languages, a shell variable is referenced differently depending on whether the variable is being directly referenced or we are asking the shell to replace the variable with its contents. In the preceding example, VARIABLE is being referenced, so it is used as it is. However, if we want the shell to replace VARIABLE with its content, we need to prepend it with $ (the dollar sign), as shown here:

```
echo $VARIABLE
```

As introduced earlier, the echo command simply prints what is given. By having the $ sign in front of the variable, we are telling the shell to replace $VARIABLE with the value assigned to it. This prints the value or data stored in VARIABLE.

Putting it all together

As we have been performing different exercises, let's begin by setting up things back to a known place. At the shell prompt, execute the cd command to go to the home directory (this is the same place you started when you first logged in), as shown here:

```
$ cd
```

There is no specific output from this command. If you are already at the home directory, this command does nothing. Now, use an editor to create a filename flash_manager.sh with the following content:

```
1: #!/bin/sh
2: OLDCOMMAND="NONE"
3: echo 999999 > /tmp/process_id
4: echo echo > /tmp/flash_command
5: dd if=/sys/bus/i2c/devices/0-0050/eeprom bs=1 skip=4 count=8 >
/tmp/bone_type
6: while :
7: do
```

```
8:      read COMMAND < /tmp/flash_command
9:      if [ $COMMAND != $OLDCOMMAND ]
10:     then
11:             read PROCESSID < /tmp/process_id
12:             if [ $PROCESSID != "999999" ]
13:             then
14:                     kill $PROCESSID
15:             fi
16:             ($COMMAND) &
17:             OLDCOMMAND=$COMMAND
18:     fi
19:     sleep 5
20: done
```

To keep exercises manageable, error checking has been omitted. In an actual product, the input should be checked for errors. As before, make sure that the execute permission is set.

Before running this, let's go through the preceding script as it introduces a few more shell scripting concepts:

- **Line 1**: This is the usual magic sequence that informs the kernel that this script is a shell script.

- **Line 2**: In this line, the OLDCOMMAND variable is set to the string NONE.

- **Line 3**: This initializes the process_id file to something invalid, so we can check for it later.

- **Line 4**: This initializes the flash_command variable with something harmless. The web page will update this for different flash options.

- **Line 5**: This gets the type of BeagleBone it is running on and saves that to /tmp/bone_type.

- **Lines 6 and 7**: These lines are infinite loops just like the ones we used in *Chapter 3, Building an LED Flasher*.

- **Line 8**: Using the read command as described earlier, we read from the /tmp/flash_command filename. The manager will receive input from the web page through that file.

- **Lines 9 and 10**: Like any other language, the shell script can perform conditional execution. Shell scripts use the if or then statements. The syntax for if is as follows:

```
if [ test condition ]
then
        [code to run if condition is true]
fi
```

The block beginning with `then` and ending with the `fi` keyword is executed if the test condition is `true`. Here, we check whether `OLDCOMMAND` and `COMMAND` are different. C programmers will recognize the meaning of `!=`, that is, not equal.

- **Lines 7 to 10**: These provide a condition whether `OLDCOMMAND` and `COMMAND` are different so that we can act on it.

- **Line 11**: This reads in the process ID from the preceding command we ran.

- **Lines 12 to 13**: These lines check whether the process ID is different from the special value we initialized it to.

- **Line 14**: If the process ID is different, we attempt to stop the preceding command with the `kill` command. The `kill` command takes the process ID and terminates that process.

- **Line 16**: This runs the command that was passed to us in the `flash_command` variable. The `&` character at the end allows this command to run in the background.

 This is potentially a big security hole. If the web page somehow manages to let a user trick it into putting anything into `/tmp/flash_command`, the user can run any command. For a real system, the content of `COMMAND` should be checked before executing.

- **Line 17**: This saves the new command, so we can detect whether there is a different command.

- **Line 19**: Using the `sleep` command, we pause for 5 seconds. A user interface can only run as fast as a person using it. Rather than checking for commands as fast as possible, we pause and try not to hog the resources.

We introduced many concepts in this exercise. We need to introduce one more for this manager. Linux is a multitasking operating system, and it can run many things at once. To run a program in the background from the shell, all that is needed is to append `&` (ampersand) at the end of the command line. This is used when we launch the LED flasher script. Without this, we would have to wait for the script to finish and would be unable to accept more commands from the web page.

The job of the manager is to watch for commands and act on it. The manager should work in the background. For testing purposes, we can run it as before. The other pieces have not been written yet, so our testing will be very basic, as shown here:

```
$ ./flash_manager.sh
```

There should be no output other than the statistics from dd, as seen earlier. Wait for a minute to make sure the loop runs. If you don't see any error messages, you have passed the basic test. We will do more testing in the next few exercises. To stop the manager, press *Ctrl + C*.

If there are any error messages, double check the typing.

Exercise 5

Now that we have a manager, let's create three scripts to flash the LEDs. These three scripts need to do the following tasks:

- A fast flash
- A slow flash
- Turn off LEDs

These scripts are very similar to the scripts we wrote in *Chapter 3, Building an LED Flasher*. Hence, we will not go through them in detail. Create each of the scripts using your editor of choice. Remember to set the execute permission on each one, as shown here:

```
flasher_fast.sh
1: #!/bin/sh
2: # Replace the names with what is used on your system
3: # Disconnect all 4 LEDs on the BeagleBone so we can use it.
4: echo none > /sys/class/leds/beaglebone:green:usr0/trigger
5: echo none > /sys/class/leds/beaglebone:green:usr1/trigger
6: echo none > /sys/class/leds/beaglebone:green:usr2/trigger
7: echo none > /sys/class/leds/beaglebone:green:usr3/trigger
8: # Start with all 4 LEDs off
9: echo 0 > /sys/class/leds/beaglebone:green:usr0/brightness
10: echo 0 > /sys/class/leds/beaglebone:green:usr1/brightness
11: echo 0 > /sys/class/leds/beaglebone:green:usr2/brightness
12: echo 0 > /sys/class/leds/beaglebone:green:usr3/brightness
13: echo $$ > /tmp/process_id
14: while :
15: do
16:    echo 255 > /sys/class/leds/beaglebone:green:usr0/brightness
17:    sleep 1
18:    echo 0 > /sys/class/leds/beaglebone:green:usr0/brightness
19:    echo 255 > /sys/class/leds/beaglebone:green:usr1/brightness
20:    sleep 1
21:    echo 0 > /sys/class/leds/beaglebone:green:usr1/brightness
22:    echo 255 > /sys/class/leds/beaglebone:green:usr2/brightness
```

```
23:    sleep 1
24:    echo 0 > /sys/class/leds/beaglebone:green:usr2/brightness
25:    echo 255 > /sys/class/leds/beaglebone:green:usr3/brightness
26:    sleep 1
27:    echo 0 > /sys/class/leds/beaglebone:green:usr3/brightness
28: done
```

flasher_slow.sh
```
1: #!/bin/sh
2: # Replace the names with what is used on your system
3: # Disconnect all 4 LEDs on the BeagleBone so we can use it.
4: echo none > /sys/class/leds/beaglebone:green:usr0/trigger
5: echo none > /sys/class/leds/beaglebone:green:usr1/trigger
6: echo none > /sys/class/leds/beaglebone:green:usr2/trigger
7: echo none > /sys/class/leds/beaglebone:green:usr3/trigger
8: # Start with all 4 LEDs off
9: echo 0 > /sys/class/leds/beaglebone:green:usr0/brightness
10: echo 0 > /sys/class/leds/beaglebone:green:usr1/brightness
11: echo 0 > /sys/class/leds/beaglebone:green:usr2/brightness
12: echo 0 > /sys/class/leds/beaglebone:green:usr3/brightness
13: echo $$ > /tmp/process_id
14: while :
15: do
16:    echo 255 > /sys/class/leds/beaglebone:green:usr0/brightness
17:    sleep 4
18:    echo 0 > /sys/class/leds/beaglebone:green:usr0/brightness
19:    echo 255 > /sys/class/leds/beaglebone:green:usr1/brightness
20:    sleep 4
21:    echo 0 > /sys/class/leds/beaglebone:green:usr1/brightness
22:    echo 255 > /sys/class/leds/beaglebone:green:usr2/brightness
23:    sleep 4
24:    echo 0 > /sys/class/leds/beaglebone:green:usr2/brightness
25:    echo 255 > /sys/class/leds/beaglebone:green:usr3/brightness
26:    sleep 4
27:    echo 0 > /sys/class/leds/beaglebone:green:usr3/brightness
28: done
```

led_off.sh
```
1: #!/bin/sh
2: # Replace the names with what is used on your system
3: # Disconnect all 4 LEDs on the BeagleBone so we can use it.
4: echo none > /sys/class/leds/beaglebone:green:usr0/trigger
5: echo none > /sys/class/leds/beaglebone:green:usr1/trigger
```

```
6: echo none > /sys/class/leds/beaglebone:green:usr2/trigger
7: echo none > /sys/class/leds/beaglebone:green:usr3/trigger
8: # Start with all 4 LEDs off
9: echo 0 > /sys/class/leds/beaglebone:green:usr0/brightness
10: echo 0 > /sys/class/leds/beaglebone:green:usr1/brightness
11: echo 0 > /sys/class/leds/beaglebone:green:usr2/brightness
12: echo 0 > /sys/class/leds/beaglebone:green:usr3/brightness
13: echo 999999 > /tmp/process_id
```

These three programs are very similar. The code to set the LEDs to a known state is repeated in each one, so they will all work the same way regardless of the order they are run. All three of these programs are modifications of the preceding exercise from *Chapter 3, Building an LED Flasher*. In each of these programs, we added line 13 to write the process ID to /tmp/process_id.

 $$ is a special variable in the shell. It means the current process ID.

The flasher_slow.sh command slows the blink rate by increasing the sleep time interval from 1 second to 4 seconds. The led_off.sh command turns off the LEDs and exits. It saves the value 999999 into /tmp/process_id so that the manager will not attempt to stop this.

As in *Chapter 3, Building an LED Flasher*, each script was run by hand to verify that it was typed correctly.

Exercise 6

In the previous two exercises, we created the backend for the user interface. The backend is the one that does the actual work. Now, we will turn our attention to the frontend. This is the part that takes the input from the user. The frontend that we will build is a simple, no-frills web page using BoneScript.

 BoneScript is a set of libraries and modules for Node.js to allow the BeagleBone to be programmed using JavaScript.

Our web page will tell the user the flavor of BeagleBone that the flasher is using, and it will provide three buttons to select a fast flash, a slow flash, or to stop flashing all together.

If you recall from *Exercise 3*, the paths used for the web server differs for Angström and Debian. Keep in mind the path used for the hello.html file from *Exercise 3*. The file for this exercise should be placed at the same place as hello.html from *Exercise 3*.

Create flasher.html at the same place where you created hello.html and type the following command:

```
1:   <html>
2:   <head>
3:   <title>Simple UI</title>
4:   <script src="bonescript.js"></script>
5:   <script>
6:   var demoRun = function(id) {
7:       var myScript = document.getElementById(id).innerHTML;
8:       myScript = myScript.replace("&lt;", "<");
9:       myScript = myScript.replace("&gt;", ">");
10:      myScript = myScript.replace("&amp;", "&");
11:      eval(myScript);
12:  };
13:  </script>
14:  </head>
15:  <body>
16:  <script>
17:      setTimeout("demoRun('getbonetype')", 500);
18:  </script>
19:  Flasher Running on <div id="bonetype">Unknown</div>
20:  <div id="getbonetype">
21:  <!--
22:  b=require('bonescript');
23:  b.readTextFile('/tmp/bone_type', showbone);
24:  function showbone(x)
25:  {
26:    document.getElementById("bonetype").innerHTML = x.data;
27:  }
28:  -->
29:  </div>
30:  <div id='ledfast'>
31:  <!--
32:  b=require('bonescript');
33:  b.writeTextFile('/tmp/flash_command', './flasher_fast.sh');
34:  -->
35:  </div>
36:  <div id='ledslow'>
37:  <!--
38:  b=require('bonescript');
```

```
39: b.writeTextFile('/tmp/flash_command', './flasher_slow.sh');
40: -->
41: </div>
42: <div id='ledoff'>
43: <!--
44: b=require('bonescript');
45: b.writeTextFile('/tmp/flash_command', './led_off.sh');
46: -->
47: </div>
48: <p>Fast LEDs flash: <button onclick="demoRun('ledfast')">Go! </
button></p>
50: <p>Slow LED  flash: <button onclick="demoRun('ledslow')">Go!</
button></p>
52: <p>Turn off LEDs: <button onclick="demoRun('ledoff')">Go </button></
p>
53: </body>
54: </html>
```

As this exercise is about creating a user interface and not about web pages or BoneScript, we will only do a cursory review of this file:

- **Line 4**: Here, we pull the BoneScript components.
- **Lines 5 to 13**: These lines execute a simple routine that run chunks of code in BoneScript.
- **Lines 16 to 18**: Here, we set up a delayed callback to run the code to read the bone_type file at /tmp/bone_type and display its contents on the web page. This is done because a few parts of BoneScript are not immediately ready.

The rest of the file creates a button for each of the three states that we want. When the button is pressed, the function in the onclick attribute is called. In each case, we call demoRun with the name of the section to execute in BoneScript. Each named section is defined by a <div id="NAME>" identifier and ends with a </div> marker. Within this, we enclose the code with <!-- and -->, so the web browser will treat it as a comment and not display it.

Testing

Provided that you have completed all the prior exercises, we can finally tie them together. Before we can use the user interface, we need to start the backend. Go to the home directory (using cd as before) and start the flash_manager.sh script, as follows:

```
$ ./flash_manager.sh
```

Navigate to the web browser as before and enter `http://192.168.7.2/flasher.html`. The following web page will appear:

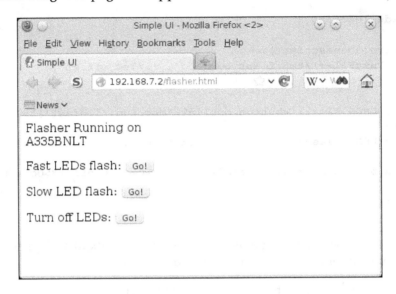

If you see a web page similar to the one shown in the preceding screenshot, give each button a try. Allow a few seconds to pass between button presses for the LED pattern to change.

Troubleshooting

If the web page does not appear, double check your typing or use a downloaded copy of the file. If the buttons don't seem to do anything, perform the following actions:

- Check your browser to make sure that JavaScript is enabled.
- Make sure that you have the `flash_manager.sh` script running. Look at the line **Flasher running on**. If it says **Unknown**, it is likely that JavaScript is not enabled.
- Assuming that you have `flash_manager.sh` running and it still doesn't do anything, check the three scripts, namely, `flasher_fast.sh`, `flasher_slow.sh`, and `led_off.sh`. They should be located in the home directory and have the execute permissions. You can exit `flash_manager.sh` by pressing *Ctrl + C*. Remember to restart it before trying again.

Exercise 7

Now that we have a flasher with a user interface to control it, let's put it all together and have it automatically start when we power on the BeagleBone.

When the BeagleBone starts up, one of the first things to run is a process manager called `systemd`.

 For the readers who are familiar with older Linux systems, this is the modern replacement for the `init` process. It does the same job as `init` and more.

The `systemd` manager's job is to start up essential system services when it first boots up. For this exercise, we will configure `systemd` to start our flasher manager. After this is done, the flasher and its user interface will run automatically each time, like a typical embedded device.

systemd takes a file that describes what needs to be run. Each thing it runs is a service. They are located at /etc/systemd/system. We will create a flasher service to start the LED flasher. While both Angström and Debian use systemd, the services are configured differently. Until now, we placed things in the home directory without having to care where this really is. However, at boot time, systemd doesn't necessarily know where things are yet, and we have to specify the actual location in the service file.

Using an editor, type the version appropriate for your system software and save the file at /lib/systemd/system/flasher.service. The commands for different users are as follows:

- For Angström users, the following service file can be used:

```
[Unit]
Description=LED Flasher
[Service]
User=root
WorkingDirectory=/home/root
ExecStart=/home/root/flash_manager.sh
[Install]
WantedBy=multi-user.target
```

- For Debian users, the following service file can be used:

```
[Unit]
Description=LED Flasher
[Service]
User=root
```

```
WorkingDirectory=/root
ExecStart=/root/flash_manager.sh
[Install]
WantedBy=multi-user.target
```

The differences between the two versions are the location of WorkingDirectory and the path to the flash_manager.sh script.

Each section of a service file is labeled by square brackets. The [Unit] section provides a readable description of what this does. The [Service] section describes what is needed to start the service. In this case, all we do is run the flash manager script. The [Install] section tells systemd under what boot up conditions does this service apply to. The multi-user.target command is the normal boot condition/state for the BeagleBone.

 In this exercise, we only use a small part of what systemd can do. For more details, refer to the documentation of systemd at http://www.freedesktop.org/wiki/Software/systemd/.

Creating the service file defines the service for systemd. To tell systemd to make use of the service, we need to enable it using the following command:

```
$ systemctl enable flasher.service
```

Testing

To test whether you correctly configured the flasher service, you need to reboot the BeagleBone. You can reboot the board by using the following reboot command:

```
$ reboot
```

Allow a few minutes for the board to shut down and reboot itself. After it finishes rebooting, go to the URL in the previous exercise. The buttons should control the LEDs.

Congratulations, you have built your first network-controlled embedded device with a BeagleBone!

Summary

In this chapter, you learned a few more features of the BeagleBone. Using what we wrote in *Chapter 3, Building an LED Flasher*, we improved it and turned our BeagleBone into a network-controlled LED flasher product.

We learned how to scan for I2C devices using low-level commands such as `i2cdetect`, read an I2C EEPROM using the Linux kernel I2C EEPROM driver, and served a web page from the BeagleBone. We also built a backend manager to support a user interface, used BoneScript to provide a web-based user interface to speak to the backend manager, and configured the Linux system software's `systemd` manager to automatically start our flasher manager on boot up.

While the LED flasher is an exercise to learn the BeagleBone, the same concepts are applicable in building other things with the BeagleBone. The important thing to remember is security considerations. They have been purposely left out to simplify the exercises. Many simple devices can be added to the BeagleBone using I2C. We will cover interfacing things using I2C and more in a coming chapter.

In the next chapter, we will turn our attention to connecting the BeagleBone to a mobile device. We will go through some of the options for connectivity and complications for each option.

5
Connecting the BeagleBone to Mobile Devices

The BeagleBone is a naturally interconnected device. Out of the box, it comes with USB networking and the Ethernet. In the previous chapter, we put together a simple network-controlled user interface for our LED flasher. In this chapter, we will look at the options to connect a BeagleBone to a mobile device. Connecting to a mobile device is an advanced task, and this chapter provides an overview of this advanced task whereas the specific details will not be covered.

In this chapter, we will cover the following topics:

- Physical connectivity options
- Android devices versus Apple iOS devices
- Phone carrier limitations
- Additional hardware
- **Bluetooth Low Energy (BLE)** and USB
- Bluetooth classic profiles (PAN/DUN)
- BLE options
- **Near Field Communication (NFC)**
- NFC options

Mobile devices

Mobile devices are a very diverse category of devices. Even the devices with the same name can be different when purchased through different sources. It is very important for anyone connecting a BeagleBone to a mobile device to never forget the diversity and evolving nature of mobile devices. A mobile device can have physical differences or adaptations specific to mobile networks or even software customizations done at the request of mobile network operators. Due to these differences, connection strategies tend to only work with a specific subset of devices; working with many devices will require multiple strategies.

Connectivity options

The BeagleBone is a very flexible device and offers many options to connect to a mobile device, such as a phone. One should not assume that connection means a full network connection; there are levels of connectivity. Connectivity can be divided into two general groups. The first is the full network connectivity and the second group is protocol-specific connectivity. There are benefits and drawbacks to each group. Most options will require additional hardware on the BeagleBone.

Full network connection options

A full network connection to a mobile device generally means a full TCP/IP connection to the mobile device. This option has the following benefits:

- A full TCP/IP connection, with the cooperation of the mobile device, can be expanded to provide Internet connectivity. It can provide access to cloud services, or with the right amount of cooperation, it can also provide services to the outside world.

- Since a TCP/IP connection looks the same to most of the applications as the USB networking and Ethernet, it can simplify software development. Any program written to work with IP networking can work with a full TCP/IP network through a mobile device almost as it is. Again, the caveat is that the mobile device and the carrier it is using need to cooperate. Under Linux, the physical connectivity is largely transparent to the application. For example, our LED flasher from *Chapter 4*, *Refining the LED Flasher*, can be made accessible to a mobile device with no changes other than setting up the connection.

- Even with limited cooperation of the network carrier, a TCP/IP connection can allow the mobile device to issue control instructions to the BeagleBone. As long as the application does not depend on the Internet or cloud services, a basic TCP/IP connection between the mobile device and the BeagleBone is all that is needed. However, the flexibility of a full TCP/IP connection comes at a price.

- A full TCP/IP connection can expose the BeagleBone to a cesspool of security issues. Unlike the Ethernet port or a desktop/laptop connected via USBnet, it is not very common to find a firewall and other security filtering on mobile devices. The application or at least something on the BeagleBone needs to take care of this or risk it being hacked. The LED flasher we built in *Chapter 4, Refining the LED Flasher*, will have to be Internet hardened. At the very least, the application should validate any inputs it receives. At the BeagleBone system software level, unused services should be disabled, and services that are required should be hardened by checking for any security updates needed and adding appropriate access controls. This is the bare minimum. Proper security-conscious design is beyond the scope of this book.

- A full TCP/IP connection depends strongly on the cooperation of the mobile device. This cooperation comes in several levels that we will address later. Some mobile devices restrict the TCP/IP connections from unapproved devices. Assuming you overcome this, there is a variety of networking issues that need to be tackled.

Protocol-specific connectivity

With less flexibility, having a protocol-specific method of connectivity can provide connectivity to a wider range of devices. The BeagleBone hardware is extremely flexible. The following are the options that can work without additional hardware:

- The BeagleBone has an onboard hardware for the USB device mode. With the right protocols, all that is needed is a cable. For device connectivity, the cable needed is the same as the one currently used to connect to a laptop/desktop but an additional adapter is needed to match the connector used on the mobile device. This requires the mobile device to support the USB host mode. Within the USB realm, things can be divided into two categories. The two categories differ in the amount of system configuration and software that needs to be written. For example, the BeagleBone system software supports the emulation of a USB serial port when the BeagleBone is connected as a USB device, so only a little configuration is needed to enable this. At the other end, a custom USB protocol can be defined, which will require you to write the system software to implement the protocol. The potential drawback of this is the lack of drivers on the mobile device.

- The BeagleBone also has hardware for a USB host mode on the board. Some mobile devices can act as a modem. This can provide access to send SMS/MMS messages or potentially even data. The BeagleBone SoC is built from the mobile device processor technology. This gives the BeagleBone in the USB host role the ability to act as a mirror.

The options with additional hardware are much more diverse. The BeagleBone has an expansion connection providing the I2C, SPI, and UART signals to provide easy interfacing with numerous options. In addition, devices can be attached to the USB host port. Examples of a few options for mobile device connectivity are as follows:

- **Bluetooth**: This can be added in several ways to the BeagleBone. The simplest way is with a USB Bluetooth adapter. A more integrated option is to use the UART signals on the expansion connector. Bluetooth opens a world of options that we'll look at later.

- **Wi-Fi**: This connection on the BeagleBone is done using the USB or SPI interfaces. This is a bit more complicated to configure. It mainly provides a wireless TCP/IP interface and potentially draws a lot of power. Wi-Fi can be run in the master mode that allows a mobile device to connect to it. However, the drawback of this is finding a suitable Wi-Fi module, as not every module will allow operation in the master mode. In the slave mode, a suitable module is easier to find but it requires considerable power at the mobile device end to emulate the master mode. You can compromise using a third device such as a mini travel router.

- **USB modules**: A mobile network USB module, such as the 3G or LTE connectivity modules, can be connected to the BeagleBone. This typically provides access to SMS/MMS and even potential TCP/IP connectivity. However, this option can be potentially very expensive. Mobile network connectivity pricing can be expensive in the monetary sense and the modules themselves can be expensive in the power consumption sense. It can potentially draw much more power than the BeagleBone.

- **NFC modules**: These can be interfaced to the I2C bus on the expansion connector. It requires a little bit more hardware and system software expertise than the USB options but a basic I2C connection requires as little as four wires. However, the data rate can be limited depending on the protocol defined.

While there are numerous options available, the rest of this chapter will mainly focus on the Bluetooth wireless connectivity options with a brief discussion of NFC.

Mobile device connections

At the time of writing this book, mobile devices can be roughly divided into two common groups, namely, Android and iOS devices. The other less common mobile devices work similarly. The biggest difference is the connectivity options offered by the device. This book will focus on discussing iOS and Android devices. The choice of mobile connectivity will be strongly influenced by the combination of mobile devices that your BeagleBone project targets.

Android devices

The core part of Android is the Android open source project built on top of Linux. As such, it has a lot of similar options and limitations as the BeagleBone. Android, acting as the system software for the phone, has built-in policy-level limitations. These limitations originate from either the design of a particular version of Android itself or from a policy of the device supplier. An added complication unique to Android devices is that the hardware can vary wildly. Android devices are built by many different suppliers, each with their own design philosophy.

The limitations and features in Android include the following:

- No Bluetooth DUN profile support. Later versions of Android add support for the PAN profile, which offers similar network functionality.

- No Bluetooth 4.0 support until Android 4.3. Even with Android 4.3, support is limited to officially supported devices.

- Bluetooth profiles support will vary greatly depending on the device manufacturer. Android runs on the Linux kernel but Bluetooth wireless support is not always implemented using BlueZ (`http://www.bluez.org/`) like on the BeagleBone. In the recent version of Android, the default Bluetooth wireless support is not BlueZ. There are different Bluetooth wireless stacks used with Android that support different amounts of functionality.

> BlueZ is the default Bluetooth stack for Linux and is provided by the BeagleBone system software.

- The options to interface using the mass storage depend strongly on the policies of the device maker.

- USB driver support will vary greatly between devices.

- Many Android 4.0 or newer devices offer NFC as a connectivity option.

- Not all Android devices support the USB host mode.

iOS devices

In contrast to Android, iOS is a closed source design. For business reasons, the device manufacturer has chosen to severely restrict the options available for connection to unapproved devices such as the BeagleBone. Everything from wireless connections to physical USB connections to software options is tightly controlled. In iOS, a TCP/IP connection to the BeagleBone requires specialized software along with the cooperation of the carrier. Bluetooth connectivity requires a special authentication process involving nonstandard hardware. However, newer versions of iOS will support Bluetooth 4.0 with the low-energy option without any special hardware. Bluetooth 4.0 (also known as Bluetooth Low Energy or Bluetooth Smart), using the GATT profile, is most likely the best option to interface with an iOS device. This will be discussed in more detail later in this chapter. In addition, except for the newest iOS-based devices, NFC is not supported.

Both Android and iOS devices can have unofficial options. For example, an Android device can be rooted to bypass many policy-level limitations. Similarly, you can jailbreak iOS devices; however useful this may be, jailbreaking will not be discussed in this book. In addition, a jailbreak can potentially invalidate any guarantees on the device.

Carrier limitations

The most interesting mobile devices to connect to the BeagleBone are phones. The network of a mobile device is subjected to specific terms, which can severely limit the options with the BeagleBone, as the terms will vary greatly from country to country and plan to plan even within the same network carrier. The following are a few issues faced:

- Restrictions on connecting another device under the same plan. This is often described as tethering. This often manifests itself as the tethering options being disabled or removed entirely from a phone. However, it can also be a contractual term. Attempting to bypass this can result in the service being suspended or terminated! It is a good idea to consult the contract terms prior to connecting the BeagleBone to a mobile device.

- TCP/IP filtering from the carrier can break applications. Included in this category are the following:
    - **Port-based filtering**: This attempts to connect to a nonstandard port for a cloud service might be blocked.
    - **Enforced proxying**: This can produce stale data or data that has been modified by the carrier.

- ○ **Limitations on the reach of certain ports**: Often, as an antispam measure, any traffic headed for the e-mail port is blocked except for those destined to the carrier's specific server, which can then authenticate or rate limit traffic.
- ○ **Connections can be one way**: The BeagleBone can make a connection to an outside service but it cannot provide services by listening to a port.

- IP addresses provided by a carrier might not be public and the address might change on each connection. This can break some services that expect both ends to know their own IP address as seen on the other end.

Bluetooth wireless technology

Bluetooth wireless technology is a wireless, short-range protocol used to interconnect devices. It can offer services that range from audio transfer to networking to a higher-level object transfer. These services make Bluetooth an ideal protocol to interface the BeagleBone to a mobile device. Due to the demand for hands-free phone functionality driven by laws, most modern phones will have a built-in Bluetooth functionality. While the BeagleBone can utilize almost all aspects of the Bluetooth wireless technology, we will focus on a few common uses of it in the context of the mobile connectivity for the BeagleBone.

 Anything called Bluetooth has to be approved by the Bluetooth SIG. Refer to www.bluetooth.org on approval requirements.

Bluetooth versions

Bluetooth wireless technology has gone through numerous revisions of the specification. At the time of writing this book, there are four major approved revisions. The versions up to 3 describe enhancements that are backward compatible. Version 4 defines a new non-backward compatible implementation designed for low power. Bluetooth 4.0 defines Bluetooth Smart. Under version 4, the protocol defined by the prior versions is Bluetooth Classic. Version 4 also defines a dual function device capable of Bluetooth Classic and BLE. The major difference with BLE is that it is designed for extremely low power consumption. This is achieved by simplifying the overall protocol.

The common names and terms relating to Bluetooth wireless technology as of version 4 of the specification are as follows:

Terms	Meaning
BLE	This is Bluetooth Low Energy defined by version 4 of the specification
Bluetooth Smart	This is similar to Bluetooth Low Energy (this is a marketing term)
Bluetooth Classic	This is the original Bluetooth protocol specified originally by version 1 of the specification
Dual role	This refers to a device that can work with both Bluetooth Classic and Bluetooth Smart devices
Bluetooth Smart Ready	This is similar to the dual role device (this is a marketing term)

Bluetooth wireless connectivity

The BeagleBone can be expanded to support the Bluetooth wireless technology connectivity without too much effort. There are a few subtle details that should be considered. While Bluetooth prior to version 4.0 is mostly interoperable, BLE in 4.0 requires specific hardware support. For general purposes, a dual role, Bluetooth 4.0 device should be strongly considered.

Linux supports many Bluetooth wireless modules or interfaces. However, the support is not universal. When selecting a module, it is best to confirm the Linux support either directly on the BeagleBone or at least on other Linux systems. If possible, determine the minimal version of the kernel needed to support the module. As the BeagleBone system software uses the BlueZ stack, it is useful to verify the compatibility. However, verifying specific compatibility with the BlueZ stack can be tricky due to vendors not understanding the request.

Profiles

The Bluetooth functionality is described in terms of profiles defined by the Bluetooth **Special Interest Group (SIG)**. There are two main profiles of interest to us and one profile is worth mentioning. There are two different profiles that offer network connectivity, namely, **Personal Area Networking (PAN)** and **Dial-up Networking (DUN)**. They both offer TCP/IP connectivity but in a different manner. It is important to repeat that network connectivity is offered by either of these options; this does not necessarily imply Internet connectivity.

Some mobile devices support the DUN or PAN profiles as a means of obtaining Internet connectivity and not exporting it. Despite this, it can still be used to provide connectivity between the device and the BeagleBone.

While we won't discuss it, it is worth mentioning **Serial Port Profile (SPP)**. SPP emulates a serial port over Bluetooth at both the BeagleBone end and the mobile device end. If TCP/IP connectivity is not needed, SPP can provide a simple connectivity. From an application point of view, this emulated serial port is the same as a regular serial port with the exception of the name.

Bluetooth profiles can be built on top of other profiles. For example, the DUN profile is built on top of SPP. So, if a mobile device supports DUN, it might also support SPP even if it is not specifically called out. The reverse is also possible with the addition of more software. For example, additional software can be added to implement the network functionality on top of SPP.

Dial-up Networking

Even if Android does not support DUN, this protocol is worth discussing. Of the two networking profiles, DUN is the simplest to implement. DUN emulates a traditional dial-up modem over SPP. A DUN connection sequence is as follows:

1. The originating end opens the emulated serial port.

2. The AT modem commands are sent to the dial string. The exact dial string depends on the implementation. A minimal implementation can ignore the dial string.

3. The originating end waits for a CONNECT response and proceeds to run PPP on the serial port.

Point to Point Protocol (PPP) is one of the common protocols used over a serial line to provide TCP/IP connectivity. The protocol is defined by RFC1661 (http://tools.ietf.org/html/rfc1661). It handles negotiation and assignment of IP addresses and other network functionalities. This can be a real TCP/IP connection or an emulated one used by some Internet connection-sharing software. An old software package called **slirp** (http://slirp.sourceforge.net/) can provide emulated functionality on Linux.

The rest of the connection is negotiated with PPP. DUN on the remote end can be added to a system that supports SPP. All that is required is software to parse the AT commands and wait for a dial string. At this point, the software responds with CONNECT and starts the PPP server.

For a BeagleBone to connect using DUN, the sequence is as follows:

1. Connect to the mobile device using RFCOMM or the DBUS interface provided by later versions of BlueZ. This establishes the underlying SPP connection. On most devices, the BeagleBone will need to be paired or pre-authenticated with the mobile device prior to this happening.

2. Open the serial port and send it a configuration and dialing sequence. The configuration sequence is specific to the carrier. Typically, this will be something like ATDT*99**. ATDT is the AT command to dial the number following the T. The number to dial will depend upon the mobile device and the carrier.

3. Wait for the other end to send a CONNECT message.

4. Then, start PPP.

After step 1, the entire process can be handled by the PPP server and its companion chat. Refer to the pppd man page for more details.

Personal Area Network

Newer versions of Android support include PAN support; so this will be the profile to use if you need a TCP/IP connection and want to work with Android devices. While DUN looks like a dial-up modem as its name suggests, PAN looks more like an Ethernet interface. It is possible to have multiple devices on a single network. While this offers more flexibility than DUN, this can be more complicated to configure. Using PAN can require some level of network design similar to an Ethernet network.

For a simple setup between a BeagleBone and an Android mobile device without taking advantage of the extra flexibility offered by the PAN profile, the configuration can be relatively straightforward. Android can be configured to export the Internet connection or it can be configured to use the connection for the Internet. Depending on the device, one or the other or both can be available. For the option to use the PAN network for the Internet, a DHCP server needs to be available on the BeagleBone and possibly a name server.

If a DHCP server is enabled on the BeagleBone and the Ethernet connection is used, be sure that the BeagleBone does not attempt to provide DHCP servers to the Ethernet side; the exception is if the BeagleBone is the only DHCP server. Having multiple conflicting DHCP servers on the same Ethernet network can lead to some very mysterious and hard-to-debug network issues!

As an example, on an Android 4.3 device, such as Galaxy Nexus, the configuration for PAN can be found in the **Settings** app. The option to export the Internet connection, if available, is found in the section under **Wireless & Networks** in the **More** option. Here, select **Tethering & portable hotspot**. Checking the **Bluetooth tethering** option will enable the PAN support, as shown in the following screenshot:

The option to do the reverse where the Android side thinks that the BeagleBone is providing an Internet access is located under **Bluetooth** in the **Settings** app. Assuming that the BeagleBone was previously paired, it should appear in the list. Select the BeagleBone's option and make sure that the box labeled **Internet access** is checked. Go back and select the BeagleBone from the list. It should attempt to connect to the BeagleBone. Note that these are typical locations of options and they can be disabled or moved by either the carrier or the device manufacturer.

For details on how to use the PAN functionality, refer to the BlueZ documentation. Be sure to refer to the documentation for the version of BlueZ used on your BeagleBone system software. At the time of writing this book, instructions that refer to using the `pand` command are obsolete. Newer versions use DBUS.

BLE options

The simplest wireless method of connecting to an iOS-based mobile device is to use BLE. Unlike Bluetooth Classic, BLE connectivity is not restricted on iOS devices. As an added benefit, Android Version 4.3 can also support BLE, provided the device has the hardware and is supported by the manufacture for BLE connectivity. BLE is not currently supported by existing mobile devices for TCP/IP connectivity.

In order to provide BLE connectivity to a mobile device, the BeagleBone needs to be configured to act as a GATT server. BlueZ contains examples of how to implement a GATT server. Refer to the BlueZ source code and documentation for more detail.

 Generic Attribute Profile (GATT) is a standard BLE profile used by a large portion of current BLE devices. This is one of the BLE profiles supported by the Android 4.3 API.

Unfortunately, at the time of writing this book, there are no simple examples of a GATT server for BlueZ.

However, if the goal is to connect to a mobile device that is designed to be used with another mobile device from the BeagleBone, there are a few examples with BlueZ. For example, if the goal is to connect to a smart watch that supports BLE and is not locked by the manufacturer, BlueZ has a library to implement the application along with a test tool. For simple tests and experiments, recent versions of BlueZ that support BLE provide a tool called `gatttool` that can perform simple operations related to GATT, such as querying an attribute. The difference between this and a BLE connection to other mobile devices is that the BeagleBone is not required to act as the GATT service.

Near Field Communication and the BeagleBone

Near Field Communication (**NFC**) is a way for new mobile devices to interact with other mobile devices, NFC tags, or to authenticate communications. NFC is not a peer-to-peer protocol. For more information on NFC, visit `https://en.wikipedia.org/wiki/Near_Field_Communication`.

Briefly, NFC works by creating a field with a low-power radio frequency transmitter on the master or server side and then monitoring it. When another NFC device or slave comes close enough to the master end, the master will see a change in the field. The roles of the master and slave can be swapped but is not necessary. Both ends communicate by controlling the way the changes occur. The following are a few key characteristics:

- NFC works over short distances. There is no numeric value for the distance as the distance depends on the antennas used by both ends. Changing the antenna has a large effect on the distance the NFC will work.

- The field provided by the transmitter can provide small amounts of power. The field power is what allows NFC tags to work. NFC tags have no power source of their own. When an NFC master comes within range, the field powers the tag and allows it to interact.

- Most NFC devices exchange small amounts of data using NFC. For example, Android devices do not send the actual applications over NFC. Instead, they send a pointer to where the application can be downloaded.

- Compared to the Bluetooth wireless technology, NFC has a comparatively low data rate.

A BeagleBone can be interfaced with NFC but, at the time of writing this book, there are very few off-the-shelf options. The options to add the NFC capability are as follows:

- **USB**: These are special devices and not the usual mass-marketed USB devices. Depending on the manufactures, drivers can be hard to find. In addition, they are often built for use with a desktop, which can mean that they have an overall size as large as the BeagleBone.

- **BeagleBone expansion boards/capes**: There are a few electrical and software options available. These typically will use the I2C or SPI interfaces on the BeagleBone to interface with an NFC chip to implement the functionality. We will talk about them in the next section.

The BeagleBone NFC expansion board options

At the time of writing this book, the author is not aware of any easily obtainable NFC expansion board for the BeagleBone. There are documented projects but the status of the board is unclear. While physically engineering an NFC expansion board is beyond the scope of this book, there are a few considerations.

The BeagleBone NFC as a device

A simple NFC device interface can be added to the BeagleBone with very little support circuitry and software. There are devices that provide a single chip with the following features:

- A standard I2C EEPROM interface from the BeagleBone side will look just like the onboard I2C EEPROM. Techniques used in *Chapter 4*, *Refining the LED Flasher*, to read the onboard EEPROM can be applied with a few minor modifications.

- An NFC interface that requires only passive components such as a coil for the antenna.

 NFC is considered to be a radio frequency technology and is regulated in many parts of the world. You should familiarize yourself with the regulatory requirements prior to implementing your own NFC interface.

ST Electronics (http://www.st.com) is a manufacturer of such a device. A simple way to test out NFC on the BeagleBone is to modify the development boards for the device.

The main considerations in software for a simple device like this are as follows:

- If you want a protocol that you would like to use to exchange information, the device provides a shared memory that is visible from I2C on the BeagleBone and from NFC

- If your protocol involves both sides writing to the memory, there should be some mechanism to avoid collisions and/or corruption of data

- These devices use the same I2C address as the EEPROM used by the capes and can potentially conflict

The BeagleBone NFC with a fully featured controller

While it is possible to use the BeagleBone as an NFC master, this can be considerably more complex. Due to the mobile device heritage of the BeagleBone, the same NFC controllers on mobile devices can often be interfaced with the BeagleBone. Using a fully featured NFC controller will offer the most flexibility. Many controllers allow both master and slave sides to be selected. There are a few drawbacks of attempting a full controller. They are as follows:

- Usually a full NFC stack is needed. Some of the work done for Android might be leveraged for a useable stack. This is needed to implement details of the NFC software protocol.

- Appropriate drivers are required for the NFC controller hardware to work with the NFC stack.

- Software to interface your application with the NFC stack.

- The hardware can be much more complicated. While communications with the BeagleBone can still be I2C or SPI, there is more complex support circuitry needed compared to the simple device implementation.

Considering how new NFC is, the Linux support for it has not been fully standardized.

Summary

In this chapter, we discussed the options and limitations of connecting the BeagleBone to a mobile device. We started by looking at the TCP/IP connection options versus non-TCP/IP options. The TCP/IP options can allow simple network interfaces similar to what we used for the LED flasher to work with minimal to no changes, whereas a non-TCP/IP option is likely to require, at the very least, application-level changes and possibly systemsoftware-level changes.

Then, we looked at options that require additional hardware on the BeagleBone and options that did not. We also covered Bluetooth wireless technology as a way of connecting to both Android- and iOS-based mobile devices. An important detail is that mobile devices are highly varied and connecting to different devices will most likely require multiple connection strategies.

In the next chapter, we will look at something more practical, such as recovering from mistakes. While no user would want their device to break, mistakes do happen. Fortunately, some of them are recoverable. We'll also discuss how to perform a few basic diagnostics and potential recovery procedures.

6
Recovering from the Mistakes

You can try to avoid mistakes, but sometimes they just happen. In this chapter, we will look at what to do after a mistake happens. While the Beagle board is designed to be robust, part of doing embedded things can involve interfacing with different hardware. Even if you haven't made a mistake before, learning the diagnostic procedures in this chapter will assist you in taking necessary precautions.

In this chapter, we will cover the following topics:

- Diagnosing different conditions with the help of LEDs
- Troubleshooting the BeagleBone with a serial port
- Repairing options

When a mistake happens, do not panic.

 For more serious mistakes resulting in a fire or injuries to you or anyone else, or anything that might threaten either you or anyone else, please contact the local emergency authorities immediately!

For less serious mistakes that do not involve an immediate threat or harm to you or anyone else, take a moment to evaluate the situation and avoid compounding the mistake with another one. This chapter makes an implicit assumption that your BeagleBone was not physically damaged. Physical damages such as torn-off connectors and cracked boards need a much more advanced evaluation of the situation.

There are several categories of problems or mistakes that can happen. In this chapter, we will try to identify the category of problems so that a reasonable recourse can be taken.

Symptoms of the mistakes

Most mistakes will lead to a few common symptoms. We will focus on the following symptoms:

- The web server on the BeagleBone is inaccessible
- SSH no longer works; you will either get an error about no such host or invalid password
- SSH appears to work, but you are immediately disconnected
- Nothing happens when you connect power to the board

The goal of this chapter is to identify problems that can be repaired with the help of software. The board is designed in such a way that it can be recovered after almost any software fault. We have intentionally not gone through the causes. For beginners, it is often very hard to identify the specific steps that lead to the problem.

Troubleshooting the BeagleBone

We will go through evaluating the board and then attempt to classify the types of problems. It is important to keep in mind that a perfect diagnosis is a difficult thing to do. The part with the LEDs can be partially done without any additional equipment. For the **BeagleBone Black (BBB)**, a serial cable can provide a lot more details.

Diagnosing with the help of LEDs

The first step is to observe the LEDs on the BeagleBone. A functional BeagleBone has a power LED light controlled by the hardware. Most BeagleBone system software will, by default, blink the other LEDs to indicate system activity. If none of the LEDs are on, check whether the power is switched on. It is especially important to verify that the BeagleBone is solely powered from the USB port. The USB specification provides up to 500 mA per port but, in some cases, this can be limited to 100 mA. The 100 mA current can cause the BeagleBone to boot and reset. Although 500 mA is available, the BeagleBone software can draw more power. It can come from the inadvertent changes to the software at the BeagleBone's end or by reconfigurations at the desktop/laptop end. If the USB power is under suspicion, try to power the BeagleBone with a barrel power connector. Note the LEDs on the BeagleBone boards. The single LED next to the barrel power jack labeled 5V is the power LED, as shown in the following image:

Setting up the serial debug cable on the BBB

For the BBB users, if you have a serial debug cable, this is a good time to use it. The **BeagleBone White (BBW)** has the serial debug cable functionality built in. If you do not have a serial debug cable, skip to the *Advanced LED diagnostics* section.

The serial to USB cable made by **Future Technology Devices International (FTDI)** will be referred to here. One end fits the 6-pin male header found between the expansion connectors (P8 and P9) on the BBB. It is placed immediately next to the P9 connector. In the following image, pin 1 is marked by a white dot at one end of the 6-pin connector; the location of the serial connector is also highlighted. If you are using the recommended TTL-232R-3V3 cable, the corresponding pin 1 on the cable is identified by a black wire.

You can see the BBB connected to the serial cable (TTL-232R-3V3) in the following image. Also, note the white dot and the black wire appears at the same end.

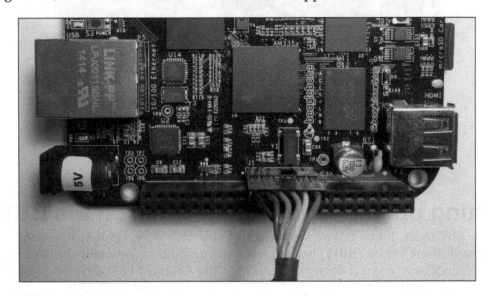

Most modern Linux distributions will have the specific drivers already installed. Windows users might need to install the drivers from the FTDI's website (http://www.ftdichip.com/).

Once installed, the BeagleBone can be accessed via the cable using the terminal software. If you are reading this chapter to prepare for mistakes rather than figuring out what to do with an inaccessible BeagleBone, it is a good idea to familiarize yourself with the serial port as it is an extremely valuable resource to troubleshoot.

Connecting to the serial port on the BeagleBone

The process to connect to the serial port is the same for both the BBW and BBB. The serial cable on the BBB and the equivalent built-in functionality on the BBW is a serial connection to the console. It's normally configured as 115200 baud, 8 bit, no parity, and 1 stop bit with no flow control. Be sure to disable the flow control in the terminal software.

On Linux, there are several terminal software choices to choose from. The example terminal software includes screen, minicom, gtkterm, or even kermit. Most of them are installable using the distribution package manager. Refer to the documentation on terminal software for more details about how to use them. One common piece of information needed by all of them is the name of the serial port.

To determine the serial port name, use dmesg and look for the name in the form of ttyUSBn where n is a number, as shown in the following command:

```
$ dmesg | grep ttyUSB | tail
[1272540.710888] usb 3-3: >FTDI USB Serial Device converter now
attached to ttyUSB0
```

The preceding command can change each time the cable is unplugged from the desktop/laptop.

> Go through this process if the cable or the BBW is unplugged. For advanced users, it is possible to configure a fixed name. For older Linux desktop/laptop systems or even newer ones with different driver configurations, the BBW provides two serial interfaces. One of them is assigned to an onboard debugger interface. For our purposes, it is usually the second one. However, if there is no output on one, try the other one.

In the preceding example, ttyUSB0 is the name of the serial port. Once you have the name of the serial port, you can connect to it with the terminal software on the laptop/desktop end, for example, with the screen command, as follows:

```
$ sudo screen /dev/ttyUSB0 115200
```

The sudo command can be optional depending on how your system is set up.

> Some desktop/laptop Linux systems might attempt to treat the serial cable as a modem if the terminal software fails to open the serial port with an error stating that it is busy; this is most likely the case. The specific details to disable this behavior will vary. Please consult the local authority for details.

For Windows users, the cable with the BBB or BBW should appear as a COM port. There are many choices of terminal software, but recent versions of the PuTTY software that we have used to log in to the BeagleBone so far can also act as the terminal software. Before using the software, you need to determine the name of the COM port. To do this, first unplug the BBB's or BBW's cable, and then start the Windows device manager. The exact location of the Windows device manager will vary depending on the version of Windows. It is usually found in **Control Panel**.

A shortcut to get to the Windows device manager for the newer versions of Windows is to explicitly run it from the **Run** dialog box, which appears by pressing the Windows key + *R*. The Windows key is usually marked with a flag such as the Windows logo. Once the **Run** dialog box appears, type devmgmt.msc and press **OK**, as shown in the following screenshot:

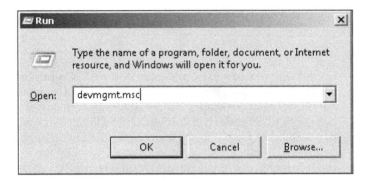

Note the choices of the COM ports. When you plug in the BeagleBone, a new COM port will appear. It might appear as a large COM port number; note it. In this example, **COM56** is the serial port name to use PuTTY, as shown in the following screenshot:

To configure PuTTY, follow these steps:

1. Start PuTTY.
2. Select **Serial** from the **Connection** options.
3. Enter the COM port name that you noted in the first box.
4. Change the **Speed** setting to 115200.
5. Change the **Flow control** to **None**. If this is misconfigured, you might still get the output, but the attempts to give an input might fail randomly. The hardware flow control signals on the BBB are not connected, and random noise can interfere with the flow control.
6. Finally, click on **Open**.

If the BeagleBone was on **COM1**, the setting will look like this:

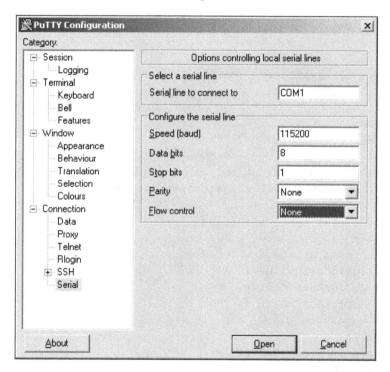

Troubleshooting with the serial port

The process for troubleshooting is slightly different between the BBB and BBW. On the BBB with the separate cable, the cable is powered by the laptop/desktop system that it is connected to. In contrast, the equivalent functionality on the BBW is powered by the BBW itself. Some early information might be lost or hard to capture.

Troubleshooting with the BBB serial port

With the terminal software running, power on the BBB and watch out for the output. A fully functional BBB will produce the following output from the U-Boot bootloader:

```
U-Boot SPL 2013.10-00015-gcbcb61f (Mar 31 2014 - 19:06:00)
reading args
spl: error reading image args, err - -1
reading u-boot.img
reading u-boot.img


U-Boot 2013.10-00016-g936eac7 (Mar 31 2014 - 19:51:25)


I2C:   ready
DRAM:  512 MiB
WARNING: Caches not enabled
NAND:  0 MiB
MMC:   OMAP SD/MMC: 0, OMAP SD/MMC: 1
*** Warning - readenv() failed, using default environment

Net:   <ethaddr> not set. Validating first E-fuse MAC
cpsw, usb_ether
Hit any key to stop autoboot:  1 ### 0
gpio: pin 53 (gpio 53) value is 1
mmc1(part 0) is current device
gpio: pin 54 (gpio 54) value is 1
SD/MMC found on device 1
reading uEnv.txt
1525 bytes read in 6 ms (248 KiB/s)
Importing environment from mmc ...
gpio: pin 55 (gpio 55) value is 1
Checking if uenvcmd is set ...
gpio: pin 56 (gpio 56) value is 1
Running uenvcmd ...
reading zImage
3688016 bytes read in 350 ms (10 MiB/s)
```

```
reading initrd.img
4539357 bytes read in 429 ms (10.1 MiB/s)
reading /dtbs/am335x-boneblack.dtb
24508 bytes read in 11 ms (2.1 MiB/s)
Kernel image @ 0x80200000 [ 0x000000 - 0x384650 ]
## Flattened Device Tree blob at 815f0000
    Booting using the fdt blob at 0x815f0000
    Using Device Tree in place at 815f0000, end 815f8fbb
```

The line `Starting kernel` marks the beginning of the output from the kernel. The following is an example of the output from the kernel on the serial port. Note that a few parts have been removed. This output is from a Debian system. Generally, the output will end with a login prompt, as shown in the following sample output:

```
Starting kernel ...

Uncompressing Linux... done, booting the kernel.
[    0.508005] omap2_mbox_probe: platform not supported
[    0.682594] tps65217-bl tps65217-bl: no platform data provided
[    0.747681] bone-capemgr bone_capemgr.9: slot #0: No cape found
[    0.784788] bone-capemgr bone_capemgr.9: slot #1: No cape found
[    0.821897] bone-capemgr bone_capemgr.9: slot #2: No cape found
[    0.859006] bone-capemgr bone_capemgr.9: slot #3: No cape found
[    0.885650] omap_hsmmc mmc.4: of_parse_phandle_with_args of 'reset'
failed
[    0.947177] pinctrl-single 44e10800.pinmux: pin 44e10854 already
requested by 44e10800.pinmux; cannot claim for gpio-leds.8
[    0.958868] pinctrl-single 44e10800.pinmux: pin-21 (gpio-leds.8)
status -22
[    0.966155] pinctrl-single 44e10800.pinmux: could not request pin 21
on device pinctrl-single
Loading, please wait...
Scanning for Btrfs filesystems
INIT: version 2.88 booting
[info] Using makefile-style concurrent boot in runlevel S.
[....] Starting the hotplug events dispatcher: udevdudevd[337]: specified
group 'fuse' unknown
udevd[337]: specified group 'fuse' unknown

[....] Synthesizing the initial hotplug events...udevd[337]: specified
user 'usbmux' unknown
[....] Waiting for /dev to be fully populated...done.
[....] Activating swap...done.
.......
```

```
Debian GNU/Linux 7 arm ttyO0

arm login:
```

Troubleshooting with the BBW serial port

As the serial port is powered by the BBW itself, the process is to connect the USB cable to the desktop/laptop. Start the terminal software. If there is no output, press and release the reset button on the BBW. The reset button is located next to the Ethernet jack near the LEDs. It will be useful if the terminal software is slow to start. The BBW might generate messages before the terminal software is ready. Reset in most cases will cause the messages to be regenerated. The location of the reset button on the BBW highlighted in black is shown in the following image:

On a normal BBW, the output after pressing reset should be very similar to the output from the BBB.

Evaluating the serial port output

The evaluation of the serial output is the same on both the BBW and BBB. If the board produces any output with more than a few characters, the most likely problem will be corrupt or missing software. If there is no output or just a single character, skip to the *No serial output* section. If there is any uncertainty, read the *Simple serial port output* section to verify that there is no serial output.

As you can get the output on the serial console, your BeagleBone is not likely to be damaged on the hardware level. All the output on the serial console is generated by some level of software. If you are in a hurry to recover the BeagleBone, reinstalling the system software as described in *Chapter 2, Software in the BeagleBone*, is a reasonable thing to do. In the following sections, we will try to further diagnose what might be wrong and make an attempt to understand the situation.

 Reinstalling the system software on the BBB will erase the onboard memory. Follow the instructions to run the software from a microSD card if you want to check whether reinstalling the system software helps. On the BBW, you can simply create another microSD card.

Simple serial port output

The most basic output from the BeagleBone is a bunch of Cs that appear on the terminal screen. This is generated by the immutable ROM bootloader on the AM335x SoC used by the BeagleBone in an attempt to solicit a download from the serial port. An example of the output from the ROM bootloader waiting for a download is shown in the following screenshot:

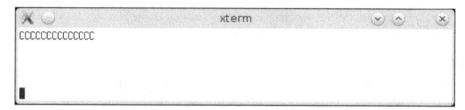

On the BBW, this happens because the ROM bootloader considers the microSD card to be invalid. This will happen if the onboard eMMC flash memory is invalid; either there is no microSD card present, or it is present but invalid. In this case, either reimage the card or fix it if it is invalid. Fixing the card is an advanced subject beyond the scope of this book. A microSD card or the eMMC flash can be invalidated due to data corruption or a direct mistake. For a microSD card, it can also be considered invalid due to poor or bad seating, so it is worthwhile to carefully eject the card and push it back in.

When the power is on, the SoC ROM bootloader checks the memory devices, which in the case of the BBB are the onboard eMMC and microSD and in the case of the BBW is the microSD. If a memory device is found, the ROM bootloader will validate it by looking at a few aspects. Only when all the aspects are found, it will consider the device valid and attempt to boot from it. The first partition is a FAT-formatted partition with a file named MLO. The MLO file has a special hash to validate its contents.

Bootloader serial port output

A prompt screen appears at the U-Boot output and the system gets as far as loading the bootloader. Refer to the first output of the bootloader in the preceding example. Normally, the second output will follow, but if the BeagleBone is stuck at the bootloader, the content similar to the second output will never show up. It should be clarified that this bootloader is different from the ROM bootloader.

Although pressing *Enter* can confirm being present at the U-Boot prompt, it can also lead to confusion. During boot up, U-Boot will look for an input from the serial console. If the input is found, the boot process is aborted. Referring back to the first output, U-Boot waits briefly for the input when it prints the message **Hit any key to stop autoboot:**.

Getting stuck at U-Boot can be a result of several things. At startup, U-Boot is configured to look for a configuration file, uEnv.txt, in the first partition. This file tells U-Boot where to load the Linux kernel from. If this file is corrupted or missing, the BeagleBone can get stuck at the bootloader level. An advanced user can search for uEnv.txt on a search engine for more details on what is needed to restore this file.

Another common way to get stuck at the bootloader level is when the Linux kernel file is missing. The location of the Linux kernel will vary depending on the version of the kernel and on the distribution used. The possible names for the kernel are as follows:

- uImage: This was the earlier/original name for the kernel
- zImage: This is a new name used for the kernel as it offers a way to incorporate configuration data in the same file

The possible locations for the kernel are as follows:

- On the first FAT partition itself under either of the two names
- Somewhere on the second Linux format partition as a system file (often in the /boot directory)

If you need to recover data from the internal eMMC flash of a BBB and your BBB got as far as the bootloader, you can search for the information specific to the distribution you are using or possibly attempt to recover the data by booting using the user button and a microSD card as described in *Chapter 2, Software in the BeagleBone*. The recovery process will require advanced system skills, so seek local assistance.

Linux serial output

If you get more text in the output, there is a possibility that Linux is running. Look for a login prompt at the end of the message or press *Enter* to see whether a prompt appears. If a prompt appears, try logging in as root just like with SSH. A successful login here most likely points to a network configuration problem. A failed login or a lack of a prompt suggests a potentially more severe problem.

For a BBB, it might be possible to boot from a microSD card and attempt to correct the problem. On the BBW, the microSD card can be removed and looked at with a reader on a laptop or desktop. In either case, further evaluation and correction is an advanced topic outside of the scope of this book.

No serial output

A total lack of serial port output points to a more hardware-oriented problem. Before going further, create a bootable microSD card as described in *Chapter 2, Software in the BeagleBone*, and attempt to boot from it. This can be done by powering off the BBB and disconnecting the USB and any barrel power connector. Then, hold down the user button when applying power. On the BBW, this is simply a matter of inserting the microSD card. This step is to eliminate a bootloader corruption, where the ROM bootloader thinks the flash is valid but is corrupted in a way that renders it useless. This also eliminates the case where the ROM bootloader is the output as described in the *Simple serial port output* section, but is missed due to the terminal software.

If the new microSD card doesn't work, the problem is most likely due to a corrupt flash. This can be repaired using the flasher image.

Advanced LED diagnostics

Assuming there is no output on the serial port with the bootable microSD card, the next step is to look at the LEDs. Look at the power LED when the power is applied. If it is off, disconnect the power. Watch the power LED as you reapply power. It might be helpful to do this in a dimmer area. If all you see is a brief flash of the power LED, there is most likely hardware damage. The power management chip on the board has detected a fault. Refer to the following section to get details about how to seek repairs.

If there is no flash at all on the power LED, verify that there is power being applied. Try unplugging all the sources of power; let the BeagleBone sit unpowered for five- to ten-minutes. There is some thermal protection on the BeagleBone and letting it stay unpowered briefly can allow the thermal protection to reset itself. If you have access to a DMM or can consult someone with access to one, verify that your power source is providing 5V to the BeagleBone. Ideally, this should be done via the barrel connector to avoid USB complications. While we have not specifically discussed expansion boards, also known as a cape, they can produce similar symptoms such as a lack of any power LED indication. Remove any expansion boards and verify the symptoms. With the 5V verified and a lack of a short flash on the power LED on a plain BeagleBone without any expansion boards, it is likely that there is a hardware component that is damaged.

Repairing the BeagleBone

After going through the previous troubleshooting process with the LEDs and the serial port, if you still do not find a fix, the next step is to look at repair options. The BeagleBone SRM document describes this procedure. Repair requests can be initiated by navigating to `http://www.beagleboard.org/support/rma`. Once approved, an RMA number will be issued and instructions to ship will be provided. The BeagleBone is then shipped back to the provided address. Depending on the nature of the problem and the length of time for which you have owned the board, there might be a cost associated with it. The concerned authorities should be able to explain this to you. Once they receive the board, they will do additional diagnostics and replace components as needed.

Since the BeagleBone is a low-cost board, the cost to ship and repair can potentially exceed the cost of a new board. For instances like this, it might be best to buy a replacement. For readers outside the U.S., they can also contact the distributor they purchased the BeagleBone from.

Summary

In this chapter, we looked at ways to recover your BeagleBone from certain mistakes. There are two primary diagnostic information sources for the BeagleBone family. The LEDs, specifically the power LED, can provide immediate information on the state of the BeagleBone. The second important diagnostic tool is the serial port. On the BBB, this requires the optional serial cable. On the BBW, this functionality is built into the board, but there are some potential sequencing problems. With these two diagnostic indicators, you should be able to fix simpler mistakes, often by just merely reinstalling the system software. This same process can also identify boards that are likely to require either a repair or replacement.

With this basic diagnostic process in hand, the next chapter will look at options to interface the BeagleBone with other hardware. If something does go wrong with interfacing hardware, the diagnostic process described in this chapter can give you some insights.

7
Interfacing with the BeagleBone

In the last few chapters, we mostly looked at the software aspects. While the BBB can do a lot by itself, it can do a lot more when connected to other hardware. This chapter will focus on general interfacing of the BeagleBone on a low level. In the next chapter, we will look at standard expansion options on a higher level.

In this chapter, we will cover the following topics:

- Electrical engineering in a nutshell
- BeagleBone voltages
- Expansion headers
- Transistors
- LEDs, relays, and switches
- I2C/SPI
- Hidden gotchas

Electrical engineering in a nutshell

This chapter is not intended in any way as a substitution for a proper education in electrical engineering! We will go over some of the fundamentals in the context of the BeagleBone so that the rest of the chapter makes sense.

Electrical properties

Electricity has three basic properties, namely, voltage, current, and resistance. Using a water analogy, voltage can be considered as the pressure and current can be considered as the rate of the water flow. Voltage is measured in volts and is written as V and current is measured in amperes and is written as either amp or A. For many of our purposes, it is convenient to measure current in milliamp or mA. This is 1/1000th of an amp. Tie this to the water analogy and amperes is the rate of charge per second. Resistance is what lets us control the amount of current or voltage. Resistance is measured in ohms.

Resistance, voltage, and current are related to each other by Ohm's law (http://en.wikipedia.org/wiki/Ohm%27s_law). It has the following three equivalent forms:

- $R = V/I$
- $V = IR$
- $I = V/R$

In the preceding formulas, R is the resistance in ohms, V is the voltage in volts, and I is the current in amps.

If any two are known, the third value can be calculated. For example, if you know the voltage and the resistance, you can calculate the amount of current that will flow through it. Similarly, if you know the voltage and want to limit the current, the preceding formula will let you calculate the resistance value.

Serial and parallel circuits

An essential concept that is needed to understand electronics is parallel and serial connections. Consider the water system in a city with a central water source. Each house gets a water feed. Except in the exceptional water usage cases, the water usage in your house doesn't affect your neighbor's house. This is an example of a parallel connection. In a parallel connection, all the connections of the same polarity are connected together. This is like the houses with all the water sources and the water drains being connected together.

For a serial connection, consider a garden hose with two valves. One valve is at the hose connection and the other valve is at the nozzle. For the water to come out of the nozzle, both the valves have to be turned on. Turning off either valve will reduce the water flow. An electrical serial connection is the same way. One device is connected to the next device in a chain such as the two valves. Resistance in either device will reduce the current through both the devices.

Measuring the electrical properties

In *Chapter 1, Introducing the Beagle Boards*, one of the recommended accessories is a **digital multimeter** (**DMM**). The DMM can measure all three properties of interest to us. Each property is measured slightly differently. Before connecting the DMM to anything, set the DMM to the correct mode and range if necessary.

Voltage measurements

Voltage is the easiest property to measure. If your DMM is autoranging where it will try to set itself based on the signal, all you need to do is put the meter in the **voltage** mode. This is commonly done by turning the knob to the **voltage** option. Sometimes this is marked with a **V** or **DCV** mark. Refer to the meter manual if it is unclear. In a manually ranged DMM, you will need to guess the voltage of your signal and select a range. When in doubt, select a higher range. For the DMM shown in *Chapter 1, Introducing the Beagle Boards*, the voltage measurement ranges are labeled **DCV** in the upper-left quadrant of the range-selector knob. The numbers on the label are the maximum voltage values for each range. For example, turning the knob to the **20** range in the **DCV** quadrant will set the meter to measure up to 20V.

 Do not attempt to measure high voltages without proper training! Consult the properly trained authority and your meter manual for details on measurements.

Once the voltage range is selected, connect the DMM to the item being measured. Voltage is measured in parallel, that is, the positive terminal of the item being measured should be connected to the red lead on the DMM, and the negative terminal of the item being measured should be connected to the black lead. There are two kinds of voltages that you might want to know about.

The first kind is the voltage being applied to the BeagleBone. For this, you connect the black lead to a ground point on the BeagleBone. Ground is the term used to refer to a reference level. The red probe will be connected to the power input. This will give you a reading for the voltage being applied. For the BeagleBone, this should measure about 5V. Anything between 5.25V and 4.75V should be fine. This is a good diagnostic to verify the power supply for the BeagleBone before using it.

The second kind of voltage measurement is the voltage across a component. Ohm's law relates current, voltage, and resistance for a component or a group of components. The resistance can be distributed over different components but Ohm's law still applies. To measure the voltage across a component, connect the meter in parallel with the component. This means placing one probe on one terminal of the component and the other probe on the other terminal of the component. The main difference here is that the probes do not need to be connected to ground.

Resistance measurements

Measurement of resistance is very similar to voltage measurement. One essential difference is that resistance is never measured with the power applied. To measure resistance, the DMM is set to a range labeled either **R** or omega (Ω) — the Greek letter for Ohm. In the example from *Chapter 1, Introducing the Beagle Boards*, the resistance range is labeled **Omega** in the lower-left quadrant. Once the resistance is set, do not connect the DMM to anything with power. A DMM measures resistance by sending a very small sense current and measuring the voltage. Connecting a DMM set to measure resistance to a live circuit can damage it. In addition, resistance in a circuit can be changed by other elements in the circuit. Unless you understand circuits completely, always measure the resistance outside a circuit. The measurement is done by connecting the DMM in parallel with the resistance element such as a resistor.

 When measuring resistance, make sure that you avoid touching the metal parts of the probes. Your fingers can influence the resistance readings.

Current measurements

Current is measured differently than voltage. Also, the DMM to measure current is connected differently than how it is connected to measure voltage or resistance. A common mistake is to attempt to measure current in parallel such as with voltage. Going back to the water analogy, current is the rate of flow. To measure the flow, you need to be in line with the flow. For electricity, the DMM will need to be in series. Measuring current is an advanced procedure. We will go through an overview of the process but do more research before attempting to measure it yourself.

Setting the DMM to measure current is very similar to setting the DMM to measure voltage. Current measurement is often labeled with **A**. In addition, some meters will require you to connect your probes to a different connector. Refer to the meter's manual to determine whether it is needed on your meter. Once set to measure current, never connect the DMM across anything like you would do to measure voltage.

Current measurement with a DMM will often require a wire to be cut. The DMM needs to be placed in series with the circuit or part in order to measure the current.

 There are advanced ways to measure current without having to cut wires. This can be done using a small sense resistor in series with the device being measured. A DMM can be set up to measure the voltage across the resistor. Current is then calculated with Ohm's law, for example, the earlier Beagle boards (not BeagleBone boards) had built-in current measurement resistors. There are other considerations beyond what can be covered in this book for this technique.

BeagleBone voltages

The BeagleBone uses a few different voltages. To prevent damage, there are voltages that should never be exceeded.

 Refer to the reference manuals and the datasheet for the AM335x SoC for the specific requirements. What is described here is a general overview. The author is not responsible for any damage to a BeagleBone! Proceed at your own risk.

The BeagleBone is designed to be powered at 5V. This is a nominal number that can vary a few percent. Attempting to power the BeagleBone with a voltage higher or lower than this will damage it or, at the very least, prevent all or part of it from working correctly. This 5V value can be provided by the barrel connector or the USB port. The USB specification limits the available current to 500mA. The BeagleBone itself can consume this much current under certain conditions. Anything being interfaced should be powered separately or the BeagleBone should be powered using the barrel connector.

The 5V power source is reduced to several lower voltages for different parts of the system. With one exception, all the digital input/output pins on the expansion connector work at 3.3V levels. This means a high or Boolean 1 is roughly 3.3V and a low or Boolean 0 is 0V. Any signals going into the BeagleBone should never be of lower value than the value of 3.3V or the voltage applied to the BeagleBone. This is important to rephase. To put it another way, do not apply any voltage to the BeagleBone if it is off! In addition, these are digital input signals, which means that the voltage applied should only be 3.3V or 0V. It is not acceptable to apply voltages between this range.

More accurately, there is an acceptable range for high and low signals. Signals outside the range are undefined and can lead to problems such as excessive power consumption. See the datasheet for the exact numbers. Generally, input values from 2 to 3.3V when the system is properly powered up will be okay as a high and 0 to 0.8V is okay as a low. Do not apply any voltage if the BeagleBone is not powered.

The exception to the 3.3V level is the analog ADC inputs on the expansion connector of the BeagleBone. They are designed for a maximum input of 1.8V. Any applied voltages should never exceed 1.8V. Unlike digital inputs, anything between 0V and the maximum of 1.8V can be applied to these analog inputs.

One important difference between the BeagleBone subfamily and the earlier BeagleBoards is the I/O voltages. On the BeagleBone, all the digital I/O is at 3.3V levels. In contrast, the earlier BeagleBoards had 1.8V I/O. Keep this in mind if you want to consider adapting projects to the BeagleBone.

If you ever need to connect a device that uses a different voltage to signal than 3.3V, consider the following few options:

- It is sometimes possible to directly interface a device with different voltages if the device provides an I/O voltage input. This input is often labeled as VDDIO. If available, check for a combination of voltages that you can use with a 3.3V I/O. For example, an accelerometer has two power inputs labeled VDD and VDDIO. Both VDD and VDDIO are labeled as ranging from 1.6 to 3.6V; however, VDDIO must be less than or equal to VDD. So, if you were to power the VDD with 1.8V, you cannot use 3.3V on VDDIO. While a device can offer the VDDIO input, breakout boards sometimes directly connect VDD and VDDIO together, effectively defeating this feature.

- Powering the device at 3.3V might be obvious but for readers used to more primitive microcontroller boards running at 5V, this might be a new option. Check the device specifications to check whether it can run the device at 3.3V. The difference between this option and the previous one is that you are powering the entire device at 3.3V, whereas the previous option only powers the I/O at 3.3V.

- Using a level converter takes the I/O at one voltage and converts it to 3.3V. Level converters are of the following three types:

    ° **Input only**: This takes the signal that is not 3.3V and converts it to a 3.3V signal used by the BeagleBone. As suggested, this is used for inputs.

    ° **Output only**: This does the opposite of the preceding converter; it takes a 3.3V signal and converts it to another voltage signal.

    ° **Bidirectional**: This attempts to automatically figure out which side is the output end and converts the other end to the same logic state but at a different voltage. These devices might not work on higher speed signals.

- For inputs to the BeagleBone, use an open collector/drain signal. An open collector/drain signal is a signal that can only drive low. It assumes that the signal is held high by some other external mechanism, such as a pull-up resistor that connects to 3.3V. For this option, it is important to confirm whether 3.3V is acceptable with the datasheet. Due to manufacturing processes, there is an upper-limit voltage for devices.

> Open drain or open collector are functionally the same for our purposes. The names refer to the type of transistor used in the chips. Strictly, open collector refers only to chips that use bipolar transistors, whereas open drain refers only to chips using FET transistors. In the rest of this chapter, we will use open collector to refer to either of these.

Expansion headers

Now that you had a whirlwind lesson on electrical engineering fundamentals, let's look at the BeagleBone side. On the BeagleBone, there are two connectors that can be used to interface to the BeagleBone. These are the same two connectors used by the expansion boards, which we will discuss in *Chapter 8, Advanced Software Topics*. This chapter will focus on some of the lower-level details for interfacing. The connector is electrically compatible between the BeagleBone Black and the BeagleBone White. However, some signals on the BeagleBone Black are shared with onboard features such as the onboard flash and the video interface. Most of these features can be disabled by following the procedures described in the BeagleBone Black SRM.

The two connectors are labeled **P8** and **P9**. See the SRM document at http://www. beagleboard.org/ for the signals and pin assignment. These connectors are 0.1 inch spaced 2 x 23 female headers. They mate with common 0.1 inch male connectors. You can see the expansion connectors' location in the following image:

The main power signals on the expansion connectors **P8** and **P9** are labeled in the preceding image. The connectors are numbered from the left-hand side to the right-hand side. The odd pins for **P9** are all along the bottom edge and the even pins for **P8** are all along the top edge. Note that the power signal comes in pairs. Signals not labeled in the preceding image are I/O or reference voltage pins.

The signals of interest in these connectors are as follows:

- A 3.3V power source. This can supply around 0.5A.
- A 5V power source if the barrel connector is used to power the BeagleBone. This can be used to power devices that have their own regulator.
- Up to 8 analog inputs. These are limited to 1.8V. Exceeding 1.8V on these pins can permanently damage the BeagleBone.
- Digital I/O that can be configured for various functions. These are 3.3V signals. They have limited current capabilities. Generally, do not pull more than 7mA for each signal. Refer to the SRM or the SoC datasheet for specific limits. We will look at how to drive things that require more power later in this chapter. The following are a few connections that we can use:

- general-purpose input/output (GPIO).

 Some GPIO signals on the BeagleBone Black are shared only for BeagleBone Black users. This is done for backward compatibility with the original BeagleBone White. This is done by connecting two or more signals together with a low-value resistor. What this means in practice is that you will need to make sure that these two signals are never set to conflicting states, such as both of them set to be outputs. If both of them are set to outputs and they are not in the exact same state (high or low), they can fight and damage the AM335x SoC.

  ° Serial interfaces such as UART, I2C, and SPI.

  ° Other more advanced features such as a video interface. See the SRM and/or the SoC datasheet for details.

The different functions on the digital lines are selected by a pinmux. Each pin on the SoC can serve up to seven different functions but only one can be exposed at a time. The pin mux allows selection of the function. Programming and configuration of the pin mux by software is being revised at the time of writing this book. Refer to the support resources of your image for the correct pin mux programming procedures. An overview of the different methods is as follows:

- The bootloader, U-Boot, can be modified to configure the pin mux. This was done in some early system software. As the Linux kernel runs after the bootloader, there is a risk of confusion from the kernel changing the pin mux.

- Older versions of the kernel allow the pin mux to be configured using board files, which are parts of the kernel specific to the BeagleBone. This requires the kernel to be rebuilt for each change and is being phased out due to this complexity.

- Some older versions of the kernel provide a debugging interface in sysfs to allow non-kernel software to program the mux.

- Newer versions of the kernel are configured by a device tree. This is the data structure used to describe the hardware at boot time. However, this interface is still being developed at the time of writing this book.

- A newer kernel specific to the BeagleBone offers a feature known as the cape manager. This takes portions of the device tree and allows them to be loaded dynamically. This is currently a feature specific to the BeagleBone and is functional only on certain versions of the kernel.

Transistors

A transistor is a key component that can allow different things to be hooked up to the BeagleBone over the expansion headers. Transistors allow things that need different voltages or more current to be controlled. A transistor has three terminals. The application of voltage or current to one terminal allows the current or voltage between the other two terminals to be controlled. This control property allows a very small signal to control a much larger signal. This has many implications for analog signals but we will mainly focus on transistors and digital signals. Other texts might refer to the transistor as a switch.

Details for the selection of transistors can be very complicated. We will go through a simplified description. Transistors can be divided into two general categories, namely, bipolar transistors and **Field Effect Transistors** (**FETs**).

Bipolar transistors

Bipolar transistors are the first type of commonly available transistors. They take a control current as the input that controls the current between the other two terminals. They have three terminals, namely, base, collector, and emitter. Application of the current through the base to the emitter will cause the transistor to set the current going from the collector to the emitter to be a multiple of the current going through the base. The multiplication is a property of the transistor and is referred to as beta. On a schematic, a bipolar transistor is drawn as follows:

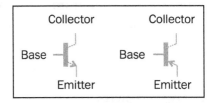

Bipolar transistors come in two versions, NPN (arrow pointing out) and PNP (arrow pointing in). They differ by the polarity of the current flowing through it.

Example use of a bipolar transistor

A common transistor for experimenting is 2N2222A or 2N3904. This is an NPN type available in an easy-to-use plastic package with three leads known as a TO-92 package, or sometimes in a small metal package. Refer to the datasheet for the lead specifics as it can vary slightly between manufactures. In this example, we will use a GPIO line on the BeagleBone to control a green LED that takes 20mA of current. The GPIO lines on the SoC can only source less than that, so we need a transistor to control the larger current. An example usage of a transistor to interface an LED to a GPIO on the BeagleBone is shown in the following diagram:

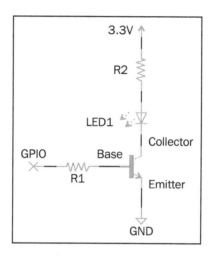

The first thing to notice in this schematic is that there are two resistors labeled **R1** and **R2**. They are required to control the current. **R1** limits the current from the BeagleBone's GPIO and **R2** limits the current to the LED. Let's work out the resistors by working from the LED back to the SoC. An LED has a property that will drop a fix voltage. For a green LED, this is approximately 2V. One end of the LED is connected to 3.3V through R2. The LED drops about 2V, so the resistor sees 3.3V to 2V or 1.3V. We want 20mA through the LED. So, using Ohm's law, we get:

1.3V/0.020A = 65 Ohm

The next resistor, **R1**, is connected between the base and the BeagleBone. The BeagleBone I/O is at 3.3V. For simplicity, let's draw 5mA from the BeagleBone.

Using Ohm's law, we get:

3.3V/5mA = 660 Ohm

Looking at a datasheet for 2N2222A, it shows a minimum beta value of 100.

 The beta value is often provided as a typical value and a minimum value. The actual value can vary a lot. When calculating, use the minimum value to ensure things can work all types of transistors.

A bipolar transistor will try to make the current from the collector to the emitter equal to the value of beta multiplied by the base current. So, in this case, *100 * 5mA = 500mA*, which is much greater than the 20mA we want. A transistor can only drop the voltage and not increase the voltage. When the actual current flowing is smaller than the current the transistor is trying for, the transistor is considered to be in saturation. For our application, this is very desirable. It means that the current will be controlled by R2.

With everything described so far, R2 might appear to be unnecessary. We could have selected R1 so that it will be multiplied to give us the required current. This is a bad idea for the following reasons:

- The beta value can vary from transistor to transistor of the same type.
- The beta value depends on the temperature.
- The calculations used earlier are a simplified approximation. Due to the way a transistor is made, the base is a diode connection and will drop roughly by 0.6V. This value changes the temperature and current flowing through it. By driving the transistor well into saturation, the exact current through the base is in material; the important point here is that there is enough current flowing to cause saturation and the current specifications of the transistor and GPIO are not exceeded.

FETs or specifically MOSFETs

The second type of transistor is a **Field Effect Transistor (FET)**. There are different flavors of FETs; the one that is of interest to us is a **Metal Oxide Semiconductor Field Effect Transistor (MOSFET)**. A MOSFET has three terminals called gate, drain, and source. A MOSFET is controlled by a voltage applied to the gate. Application of voltage to the gate causes the current between the drain and source to change. A MOSFET can be tricky for a beginner to use. We will go through an overview but specific details are beyond the scope of this book.

Unlike the base on a bipolar transistor, the gate on a MOSFET is an open circuit. No steady current flows through the gate. The advantage is that we save a part, as we do not need a resistor to control the current. The drawback is that the gate itself is a very thin layer of glass that can be damaged by static electricity. A MOSFET should be kept in the protective material it was shipped in until it is ready to use.

What makes the MOSFET more complex to use is the drain source path is not controlled by a simple multiplier. MOSFETs have a gate threshold voltage before the drain source path is affected. In addition, the effect on the drain source path depends on the type of MOSFET. It can increase or decrease the current, unlike a bipolar transistor. Once a MOSFET is properly selected, it can be used in a similar manner.

Connecting LEDs to the BeagleBone

We made many references to **Light Emitting Diodes** (**LEDs**) in this book and many readers are interested in LEDs. They can serve both decorative and functional purposes. LEDs are diodes that light up as the name suggests. Diodes are two-terminal, one-way electricity controls. Current is allowed to flow only in one direction. The important characteristics of LEDs are as follows:

- They have a minimum voltage before they can turn on. This voltage will vary slightly with the amount of current flowing through it. Different LEDs will have different voltages. This is determined by the underlying physics of the LED. On a datasheet, this is often labeled as the forward voltage.

- As an LED is a diode which conducts only in one direction, the polarity at which an LED is hooked up matters. The terminals on an LED are the anode and the cathode. The anode should go to the positive side of the power source.

- The brightness of the LEDs is determined by the current through them. An LED always needs a resistor or some other means of limiting the current. The recommended and maximum currents through an LED are specified in the datasheet for the LED. Generally, an LED will require a minimum current before it lights up. Then, it will get proportionally brighter as the current increases up to a point. Beyond this point, increasing the current will not proportionally increase brightness and might damage the LED.

- Some LEDs are rated for use in a multiplexing operation. Multiplexing is a way of controlling a large number of LEDs without having to use exactly two wires per LED. This is usually done by turning on LEDs one at a time. However, as the LEDs are not continuously on, they can appear dim. The solution is to drive the LED with a large current pulse for a brief period of time. This is the multiplexing or pulsed current rating. This rating is usually specified with a maximum duration.

Most LEDs will require a transistor to drive. The considerations to drive the LEDs are as follows:

- For a first approximation, the forward voltage of an LED depends on the color of the LED. Red, yellow, and some green LEDs tend to have a forward voltage of around 2V or less. Blue and white LEDs have higher forward voltages in the range of 3.0V to 4.0V. Unless you specifically look for a blue or white LED of lower forward voltage, you will need a higher voltage than 3.3V.

- Current through an LED controls its brightness. However, varying current with software can be difficult. A common way to control the brightness is to flash an LED faster than the human eyes can see. By varying how long an LED remains on before turning off, the LED can appear to be at different brightness. This technique is called **pulse width modulation (PWM)**. The BeagleBone can do this by software or hardware.

Controlling relay with a BeagleBone

While a transistor can be used to interface with devices that require more current or a higher voltage, a transistor is still electrically connected to the BeagleBone. A relay is a mechanical switch that is activated or deactivated by an electromagnet and can provide electrical isolation. There are a few potential hazards with controlling a relay. This applies to anything that has a coil such as a solenoid, motor, or even an electromagnet. As a group, they are known as inductive loads. Without going into the physics, switching an inductive load can result in voltage spikes, known as an inductive kickback, which can damage the transistors. The following are the points to consider when connecting to a relay:

- Consider the current required by the relay. Compared to LEDs, relays can require more power. Check the relay specifications. Sometimes, relay specifies a coil resistance. You can use Ohm's law to figure out the current needed to drive it.

- Relays come in a variety of voltage ratings. Except for the lowest power relays, relays can require voltages higher than 3.3V.

- There are dedicated chips to drive relays but for a simple low-power driver, a transistor can be used.

- When using a transistor or a dedicated driver that does not include protection against the inductive kickback, you will need to add a diode in parallel with the relay. The diode is connected such that when the relay is turned on, current does not flow through the diode. However, when the relay is turned off, the inductive kickback is shunted through the diode. This works because the inductive kickback occurs in the opposite polarity. The following diagram shows the sample relay interface. The **D1** diode handles the inductive kickback when the relay switches off.

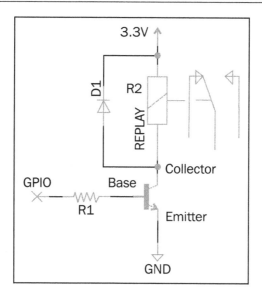

Connecting switches to the BeagleBone

So far, we have mostly looked at outputs from the BeagleBone. Let's look at getting the physical input. The switches that we are talking about here are simple mechanical devices that can open or close a circuit. They can be push button switches such as the user or reset button on the BeagleBone, or they can be slide switches. They can also be sensors. For example, you can detect tilt by having a metal ball sitting between two wires in a box. When the box is tilted, the ball rolls away and opens the circuit. All of these are interfaced similarly. One important thing to remember is that these switches are passive. They do not have power. The following diagram shows a sample switch connection (**SW1**) to a GPIO:

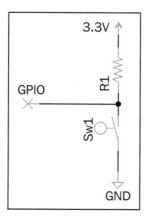

A passive switch can be connected to the BeagleBone's GPIO by connecting one terminal of the switch to ground and the other end to 3.3V through a resistor. The GPIO is connected to the resistor on the side connected to the switch. The resistor is large enough, so when the switch is closed, not too much current flows. It needs to be small enough, so the noise doesn't interfere. The common values that work for this are between 1000 to 4700 Ohms.

I2C/SPI on the BeagleBone expansion connector

I2C and SPI are two common serial buses used to interface with many commonly used peripherals. Using these buses while interfacing is more advanced than a simple beginner's task; beginners should be aware of them. In our exercises, although we looked at I2C, we focused on what is on the board itself.

Inter-Integrated Circuit

Inter-Integrated Circuit (I2C) is a two-wire serial bus interface. This interface defines a full protocol to allow different devices on the bus to be identified with addresses. Different combinations of the states of two wires are used to identify different parts of the protocol. When using I2C to interface from the BeagleBone to an I2C device, the key things to be aware of are as follows:

- I2C signals are open collector. This allows multiple devices to be connected in parallel. However, this requires two resistors, roughly from 1000 to 4700 Ohms that connect each of the I2C signals to 3.3V. Open collector means each device can make the signal low but not high. This way if two devices try to transfer data at once, there will be no electrical damage.

- I2C signals can be bidirectional. The same wires can have data flowing in and out of the BeagleBone.

- I2C is half duplex. At any given time, data can flow in only one direction.

- I2C devices can work with different voltages. On the BeagleBone, this is 3.3V. In the event that you need to convert between voltages, keep in mind that you will need a bidirectional converter.

Serial Peripheral Interface

Serial Peripheral Interface (SPI) is a three-wire serial interface. This is a very simple serial interface. In contrast to I2C, the SPI interface only defines bits and has no concept of bytes. It can be considered to be a shift register. The device being connected to will have additional constraints on the data format it wants.

The three wires or signals are as follows:

- **Clock**: The data is transferred either on the rising or falling edge of the clock. The edge used depends on the device.

- **A signal to transfer data from the BeagleBone to the device**: This is sometimes known as **Master Out Slave In (MOSI)** or **Slave In Master Out (SIMO)**. The master is the BeagleBone and the device is the slave. This line can be optional for write-only devices such as an SPI control for an LED. The clock-edge configuration determines when data is valid on this line.

- **A signal to transfer data from the device to the BeagleBone**: This is sometimes known as **Master In Slave Out (MISO)** or **Slave Out Master In (SOMI)**. The master is the BeagleBone and the device is the slave. This line can be optional for read-only devices such as a dumb sensor that provides data. The clock-edge configuration determines when data is valid on this line.

On each tick of the clock, both the BeagleBone and the device will each receive and transmit one bit. SPI is always a full-duplex interface. Data flowing on either wire can be ignored by either side but cannot be stopped. SPI is commonly used with one additional wire, a chip select (http://en.wikipedia.org/wiki/Chip_select) or an enable signal. This is the signal that tells the device you are connecting to that it is being talked to. It is optional but not using this signal means you can only have one device per SPI interface. This signal is normally an active low signal on the BeagleBone. An active low chip select means the chip select signal only enables the device when the signal is low or logic 0.

An example connection using the chip select signal is to connect the clock, MOSI, and MISO in parallel. Unless the chip select signal is active, the slave device keeps its MISO signal tristated, that is, the signal is put into a state as if it was not there. The slave device also ignores the clock and MOSI line while the chip select signal is inactive. When the chip select signal is active, the slave device responds. This way, the master can select which slave device to talk to.

Summary

In this chapter, we went through a quick description of basic electrical engineering concepts as a foundation for interfacing the BeagleBone with other things. We looked at the available signals and power on the expansion connectors, P8 and P9, on the BeagleBone. We also briefly looked at the pin mux used to select different functionalities on the expansion connector. For the expansion connector, we discussed several details that are critical for interfacing. The BeagleBone uses 3.3V for all the logic signals. The only signals that aren't 3.3V on the BeagleBone are the 1.8V analog to digital converter inputs. We then looked at using a transistor to interface to signals that aren't 3.3V and to drive higher current.

We also looked at a few specific things that can be interfaced using a transistor. For the LEDs, we looked into determining the resistor values using Ohm's law. For relays, we touched on hazards such as inductive kickback, which can be suppressed with a diode.

Then, we turned our attention to taking input from a switch with a pull-up resistor on a GPIO. Finally, we got a taste of interfacing with SPI and I2C buses. We looked at the signals involved for each bus.

In the next chapter, we will discuss expanding the BeagleBone on a higher level using expansion boards and off-the-shelf accessories.

8

Advanced Software Topics

So far, all of our programming has been done using high-level languages, such as shell script or Node.js. In this chapter, we will look at other BeagleBone software development methods along with other pieces of software on the BeagleBone that are necessary to support additional hardware. The BeagleBone is a full Linux system like Linux on a desktop or laptop and most desktop development techniques will be applicable. In this chapter, we will cover the following topics:

- BeagleBone programming with the C and Linux APIs
- User space / kernel space
- Kernel driver on the BeagleBone
- Device tree on the BeagleBone
- Pinmuxing
- Real-time behavior on Linux

The BeagleBone programming with the C and Linux APIs

Almost all Linux programs written in C for a desktop or laptop can be made to work on the BeagleBone if it uses only the Linux API. While this is a qualified statement, many programs will fall into this category. The gating factor is the presence of hardware. For example, a program that requires a keyboard will not work unless a keyboard is installed.

 This section is applicable to other programming languages such as C++.

The things that are likely to break when moving from the desktop to the BeagleBone are as follows:

- Software that accesses hardware using the low-level APIs rather than the higher-level abstractions layers; for example, an older desktop system may offer a parallel port that some applications will try to use as GPIOs. While the parallel port access is a standard Linux API, there is no equivalent parallel port on the BeagleBone.

> Most software written to use the parallel port in this fashion can often be rewritten to use the GPIO on the BeagleBone. The primary concern in this case is the electrical interface. A PC parallel port usually runs at 5V, but the BeagleBone GPIO runs at 3.3V.

- Using the desktop-specific features such as interfacing to the PCI and PCIe buses. These buses do not exist on the BeagleBone. Most likely the bus-specific software is trying to determine features such as address and mapping, which can be done on the BeagleBone but in a different manner. This is another example of using a low-level API instead of a proper Linux kernel abstraction.

- Software that makes assumptions about memory alignment is not likely to work. The x86 architecture used on a desktop Linux has hardware support for unaligned accesses. The ARM architecture on the BeagleBone will generate a fault on unaligned access. This is likely to appear as a segmentation fault or a performance impact if Linux is configured to emulate the unaligned access. An example of the unaligned access is casting an offset in an array of `char` into `int` without checking the word's boundary alignment.

- Multimedia acceleration may range from suboptimal or completely broken when moved directly to the BeagleBone. This is due to the differences in SIMD instructions on the x86 versus the ARM cores. Often this will break immediately due to the acceleration being written in machine language, but this may be a potential problem if it is done with the C code and assumptions on the compiler.

> The ARM core on the BeagleBone has an SIMD instruction set known as NEON. It is designed for multimedia acceleration but requires the software to be written for it.

- 3D graphics program written to use the full OpenGL API. The BeagleBone hardware only supports OpenGL ES, which is the embedded subset.

The preceding issues on the BeagleBone are largely due to hardware differences. The BeagleBone uses an ARM core whereas desktops and laptops mostly use an x86 core.

The reverse, running the BeagleBone Linux C program on a desktop or laptop, is less likely to work for several reasons. The important things to keep in mind when trying to prototype software on a desktop or laptop for the BeagleBone are as follows:

- Interfacing many types of hardware with the BeagleBone is relatively straightforward. However, this is less straightforward on a desktop. BeagleBone software is commonly written to control the hardware attached to it. For example, most desktop systems do not offer GPIOs unlike the BeagleBone. Software written to control GPIOs is not likely to work.

- It is easy to abuse Linux APIs as a shortcut to avoid writing proper drivers, but this will break prototyping software on desktops. An example is the common circulated shortcut to directly configure the BeagleBone hardware by reading and writing to /dev/mem. Reading and writing to /dev/mem is a Linux standard API but the behavior is very specific to the BeagleBone. For almost everything, the same task can be done by proper higher-level Linux APIs or writing a proper Linux kernel driver.

- An exception to this is the higher-level applications that tend to be very portable. The graphical user interface can often be moved between the desktop and the BeagleBone provided they use the same underlying framework. For example, an application with a graphic display using the X Windows system should work with almost no changes on the BeagleBone provided a proper X server is installed.

Building the BeagleBone applications with the Linux API

Except for simple applications, most applications will leverage the existing libraries or even existing applications. The rich library of Linux applications is a very strong reason to use Linux in an embedded device such as the BeagleBone. This can be done in two general ways. The library may be available from the system software provider. For example, the Debian-based and Ubuntu-based distributions on the BeagleBone offer most of the same libraries as the equivalent on a desktop. The second way is compiling the library yourself.

Compiling the existing libraries on the BeagleBone

In general, libraries can be natively compiled on the BeagleBone just like on a desktop. Most distributions for the BeagleBone will have a C compiler installed by default along with standard header files. The tools to compile software not included beyond the C compiler can usually be installed from the distribution's repository. There are a few drawbacks of native compilation on the BeagleBone. They are as follows:

- **Speed**: As flexible and as powerful as the BeagleBone is, most desktop systems are faster. This translates into a quicker compilation compared to the BeagleBone.

- **Storage space**: The BeagleBone is designed to be an embedded device and lacks high-speed interfaces for hard drives. At the time of writing this book, the primary storage space on the BeagleBone is the microSD card, which is limited to about 32 GB. Most modern hard drives can easily exceed this capacity. The USB interface can be used for a hard drive interface, but this is of limited speed.

- **Memory**: The BeagleBone has considerably less memory than the current desktop systems. A BeagleBone Black with 512 MB has between 1/8 and 1/32 of the memory on a desktop system. Lack of memory can limit compilation speed more than a slower processor.

Cross compiling software for the BeagleBone

One way to side step the preceding limitations is to cross compile software. Cross compiling software is the process of compiling software on a desktop or a laptop using a special compiler to generate binaries suitable for the BeagleBone. Cross compiling takes advantage of the faster and resource-rich desktop system to generate software for embedded devices that have fewer resources. Cross compilation terminology describes the host as the machine running the compiler. The target is the machine that will run the resultant executable. In our case, the host is the desktop machine and the target is the BeagleBone. This extra speed does come with some added complications as follows:

- A special cross compiler is needed. The easiest way to obtain a cross compiler is to install one from the distribution on the desktop. This can also be downloaded from http://www.linaro.org/downloads/. Look for the section labeled *Toolchains*. Toolchains can also be built using a script called crosstool-ng. Check out the link http://crosstool-ng.org/ for details.

- For libraries designed to use build wrapper tools such as `cmake`, `libtools`, or `autoconf`, special parameters will need to be provided to the wrapper tool to make them aware of cross compilation. Unfortunately, some packages have not been tested with cross compilation or worse yet, written in a way that uses these tools that make cross compilation difficult. An example problem is an `autoconf` configure script that explicitly tries to build and run the resultant executable using the cross compiler. A cross compiler for the BeagleBone will generate binaries suitable for ARM, which will not run on a desktop.

- Library build systems that make assumptions on locations can have subtle, hard-to-detect bugs. For example, a library build system has an explicit reference to look for headers at `/usr/local/include` rather than allow the path to be supplied. Using `/usr/local/include` will pick up the `include` files configured for the host system rather than the proper target system's `include` files.

There are several tools designed to work around these complications. These tools are often used by the distributions to build (for more details, use a search engine):

- **Buildroot**: This is one of the simpler tools but is not currently used much. It is a collection of makefiles to help with cross compilation. For more details, visit `http://buildroot.uclibc.org/`.

- **OpenEmbedded and Yocto**: These two share a common foundation but offer different degrees of support. They are extremely powerful tools for cross compilation. Other extremely advanced features include the ability to build a fully customized image for flashing with a single command. OpenEmbedded is the tool used to build the Angström distribution. The flexibility and power of OpenEmbedded comes at the price of slightly more complex configuration and a steeper learning curve. OpenEmbedded offers a full collection of build tools and cross compilation configuration to work around the complications. In addition, OpenEmbedded has a large number of recipes to handle cross compilation of many packages. For more information, visit `http://openembedded.org/`.

> OpenEmbedded is a build tool and is often confused with distributions. OpenEmbedded can be used to build different distributions. For example, Angström is a distribution built using the OpenEmbedded tool. A distribution is a collection of different pieces of software with a configuration scheme defined by configuration files within OpenEmbedded.

Examples of the BeagleBone C compilation

To illustrate C compilation for the BeagleBone, we will once again use the classic `Hello, World` example. The code shown below can be used to check the distribution and toolchains:

```
1: #include <stdio.h>
2: int main(int argc, char **argv)
3: {
4:     printf("Hello, World\n");
5:     return 0;
6: }
```

Put this program in a file named `hello.c` on the build system.

Native BeagleBone compilation

To compile the preceding program, use the following command:

```
$ gcc hello.c -o hello
```

To test the resultant executable, use the following command:

```
$ ./hello
```

If the compiler is working, there should be no errors; errors such as command not found or missing `stdio.h` points to the distribution not having the compiler or header files properly installed.

Cross compiling a program for the BeagleBone

Make sure your cross compiler is installed on your desktop or laptop. This example assumes you are on a Linux system. Cross compiling from a Mac or a Windows system is possible but will not be covered in this chapter. The name of the cross compiler will vary depending on which cross compiler you are using. Generally, the cross compiler will be named something like this:

```
arm-none-eabi-gcc
```

The name will typically begin with `arm` and end with `gcc`. The wording between `arm` and `none` will vary depending on the source of the compiler. Everything from `arm` up to the dash before the `gcc` is known as the cross compilation prefix. One trick to identifying the cross compiler if it is installed in the search path is to type `arm-` and invoke the shell's completion feature with the *Tab* key. If it is set up correctly, this will often show enough information to determine the cross compiler prefix.

A potential trap for cross compiling is the cross compiler must be configured to use the same libraries as the distribution used on the BeagleBone. It is possible to have a cross compiler set up to generate ARM binaries but not call the correct libraries. Examples of cross compilers that can cause problem are as follows:

- The older BeagleBone distributions came in two flavors reflecting the libraries they were configured for. Older ARM cores did not include floating point support in the hardware, so all the floating point operations had to be emulated. As floating point support was added to the ARM core, the additional support was invoked by the emulation code. This is inefficient as it requires additional steps. This process is described as soft float. A high performance method of invoking floating point support is to directly generate code that would fail on systems that are not equipped with floating point. This method is hard float. A compiler configured to use hard float binaries is not compatible with a BeagleBone distribution setup for soft float and vice versa.

- Android systems use a simplified library known as bionic. A cross compiler, such as the one that is provided with the Android native development kit, will not properly compile programs for a BeagleBone. An obvious exception is if the BeagleBone is running Android!

- The BeagleBone uses an ARM Cortex-A8 core. Other embedded devices can have ARM cores, such as a Cortex-M0, Cortex-M3, or Cortex-M4. The cross compiler setup for these cores is incompatible with the BeagleBone.

Unfortunately, there are no universal ways to determine cross compiler suitability. The original intent of the cross compiler name is to identify how it was configured. However, many cross compilers are vaguely named with no definitive indication of compatibility.

To cross compile for the BeagleBone after installing the cross compiler, use the following command:

```
arm-none-eabi-gcc hello.c -o hello
```

Replace the prefix if your cross compiler has a different prefix. The native compiler and the cross compiler share the same arguments provided they are from the same version of the compiler. You can determine the compiler version using the -v option, as follows:

- For a native compiler, use the following command:

```
$ gcc -v
```

- For a cross compiler, use the following command:

```
$ arm-none-eabi-gcc -v
```

It is very important to ensure any path reference contain suitable files for the BeagleBone. For example, if the `include` file search path option (`-I`) or the library search path option (`-L`) is used, only point them to versions for the BeagleBone. It is unlikely to be `/usr/include`, `/usr/lib`, `/usr/local/include`, or `/usr/local/lib`.

The executable generated earlier can be tested by following these steps:

1. Copy `hello` to the BeagleBone using `scp` as described in the exercises earlier. For example, the following command will copy it to `/tmp` on the BeagleBone:

   ```
   $ scp hello root@192.168.7.2:/tmp
   ```

2. Then, execute it using the following command:

   ```
   $ /tmp/hello
   ```

One common but confusing error is **File not found** while attempting to execute it. If `ls -l` shows the file with the right permissions, then the likely common problem is that the cross compilation toolchain is not configured for the distribution used on the BeagleBone.

> By default, executables are dynamically linked. During compilation, the name of the dynamic linker is hardcoded into the executable. If this name does not match the dynamic linker on the BeagleBone, the system will complain about the file not found. This error refers to the dynamic linker not being found.

User space versus kernel space on the BeagleBone

On Linux, software is divided into two realms. The first realm, kernel space, is a privileged space that has visibility of the entire system. On some systems, this is also known as the supervisor mode. The other realm, user space, is an unprivileged space backed by hardware. It has a limited visibility of the entire system. All hardware access is done through the Linux API. Attempts to increase visibility beyond what the Linux API allows will result in a fault or at least an error. All the exercises up to this point have been exclusively in the user space. One important detail to note is that the system software or distributions include both kernel and user space components. Kernel space is exclusively in the Linux kernel and everything else is user space.

The distinction between user space and kernel on the BeagleBone is very important. The kernel is aware of the differences in hardware. A few things that the kernel is aware of are as follows:

- **Board level bugs or feature changes**: If the future version of the BeagleBone changes the way the LEDs are used in our LED flasher exercises, the kernel will have to know about it. Similarly, if the BeagleBone contains different revisions of the hardware, the kernel will have to be aware of it too.

- **Errata and fixes on the SoC**: The SoC is a complicated piece of silicon and has errata associated with it. For example, the initial BeagleBone White boards contain the first revision of the AM335x SoC rated at a maximum 720 MHz. The BeagleBone Black uses the second revision of the same SoC rated at 1 GHz. The kernel at boot time detects the revision and sets the clock's speed limits appropriately.

- **Physical resources on the system**: The memory on the BeagleBone Black and BeagleBone White differ in size and type. The kernel is aware of it and does its best to abstract the difference away from user space.

The benefit of the kernel being aware of these differences is that the user space software can often be agnostic to the differences. Our LED flasher exercises will work on future boards as long as the kernel presents the same interface.

For most users, the following key points apply:

- User space offers more debugging tools compared to the kernel.
- User space has the illusion of multitasking so it is very easy to open multiple sessions to the BeagleBone when debugging.
- Due to abstractions, user space can have performance penalties.
- User space depends on hardware support being in the kernel.
- It is very tempting to use the debugging Linux APIs to circumvent the user space limitations to support new hardware or to avoid learning the proper API. This is a very bad idea for the following reasons:
  - It makes the user space application specific to the revision of the hardware
  - This discards any protections offered by abstracting the hardware
  - It makes it very difficult to move to improved hardware, for example, this would complicate movement from the original BeagleBoard classic to the BeagleBone
  - Debugging APIs such as `spidev` or the equivalent for I2C were created to debug without performance considerations

Kernel drivers on the BeagleBone

The proper means to support hardware on the BeagleBone is with a Linux kernel driver. This includes both stock hardware on the BeagleBone and any new added hardware. Using a kernel driver avoids the preceding drawbacks and allows maximum performance benefits. The resources on the SoC can be used with minimal difficulty. Access to things such as DMA and interrupts are very difficult in user space but are relatively straightforward in the kernel.

Writing a device driver is beyond the scope of this introductory book. However, advanced beginners should be aware of how to build the kernel. The Linux kernel is well written and cross compilation is easily done. Building the kernel can be done in a series of steps. You will need a cross compiler. The sample command lines assume the cross compiler prefix is `arm-none-eabi-`. If you have a different compiler setup, replace that prefix with yours. All the following commands will have `ARCH=arm` to tell the kernel build system that you are building for the ARM architecture.

These instructions assume you are cross compiling from a Linux desktop or laptop. It is possible to compile the kernel natively on the BeagleBone, but it can be a long and tedious process. For those who would like to attempt it, the same instructions can be used with the cross compile prefix set to empty or by just omitting the `CROSS_COMPILE=` part entirely. Kernel compilation is generally not supported on other operating systems such as Windows. For users on Windows, the easiest option is to create a virtual machine running Linux.

 Some distributions have the process partially automated with a script. For example, the Angström kernel is built by the OpenEmbedded build system. The Debian BeagleBone kernels can be built using the process described at `http://eewiki.net/display/linuxonarm/BeagleBone`. This build process uses a script to automate the building.

To build the Debian BeagleBone kernels, follow these steps:

1. Download the kernel source tree. The core support for the BeagleBone is in the mainline Linux kernel but other trees specific to BeagleBone may offer more functionality. Kernel trees are often provided as part of a Git repository. Git is a source revision control system commonly used by Linux kernel developers. If the kernel is not in a Git repository, unpack the download.

2. Navigate to the kernel tree you have downloaded. This is usually a directory with folders such as arch, boot, drivers, kernel, and other. Depending on how you download the kernel tree in the last step, the place you need to be buried is in a directory or two deep. The rest of the instructions assume that you are in the directory with the subdirectories. You will need to create a configuration file. There are two common ways to get a configuration file. They are as follows:

    ○ If the kernel source you are using is similar to your running system and your running system provides it, you can then copy the compressed configuration file from your BeagleBone. The compressed configuration file is at /proc/config.gz. For example:

    ```
    $ scp root@192.168.7.2:/proc/config.gz /tmp
    $ gzip -d /tmp/config.gz
    $ cp /tmp/config TOP_OF_YOUR_KERNEL_TREE/.config
    ```

    If your kernel tree is at /home/user/BeagleBoneKernel, replace TOP_OF_YOUR_KERNEL_TREE with /home/user/BeagleBoneKernel.

    ○ Attempt to use the default config file. Depending on the kernel tree, this may be potentially buggy. To use the default configuration, use the following command:

    ```
    make ARCH=arm omap2plus_defconfig
    ```

    This will set the configuration to the default configuration. The kernel configuration file is stored in .config on the top of the kernel tree.

3. Optionally, edit the configuration file as necessary. New drivers can often be added by just enabling the option. There are several interfaces to configure the kernel. You can invoke them using the following command:

    ```
    $ make ARCH=arm menuconfig
    ```

    This will start a text-mode, graphical-like interface.

    ```
    $ make ARCH=arm xconfig
    ```

    This will start a graphical interface that can be used with a mouse. It is strongly recommended that you use one of these options to edit the kernel configuration. While the config file is a text file, manual edits may not correctly manage all the dependencies for a given option.

4. To build the kernel, use one of the following two commands. The difference is the format used by the distribution.

    ° For newer versions of Ubuntu/Debian, use the following command:

    `make ARCH=arm CROSS_COMPILE=arm-none-eabi- zImage`

    The resultant kernel will be at `arch/arm/boot/zImage`.

    ° For Angström, use the following command:

    `make ARCH=arm CROSS_COMPILE=arm-none-eabi- uImage`

    The resultant kernel will be at `arch/arm/boot/uImage`.

5. The `-j` option can be safely added to the `make` command line to parallelize the compilation. However, this hides compilation errors.

6. If your kernel is configured to use `modules`, they can be built by the following command:

    `make ARCH=arm CROSS_COMPILE=arm-none-eabi- modules`

7. Install the kernel. The exact location of the kernel will depend on the distribution of the system software that you are using. As this is beyond the scope of this book, refer to the distribution for details on where to place the kernel and the name for it.

> As a precaution, save the old kernel in case your new kernel has problems. This can be done by renaming the original `uImage`/ `zImage` image before copying into your kernel. On the BeagleBone White, you can revert to the original kernel using an SD card reader on the desktop. For the BeagleBone Black, you can boot from a microSD card like you do on the BeagleBone White, and then manually revert the change on the internal flash. Alternatively, experiment with new kernels using a microSD card.

Device trees on the BeagleBone

One feature that was introduced in the Linux kernel is the concept of a device tree. The goal of the device tree is to allow one kernel binary to support different hardware by changing the device tree. A device tree is a data structure used by the kernel to describe the underlying hardware.

The device tree data informs the kernel about the following:

- Physical address of the hardware blocks, for example, the I2C block on the BeagleBone is supported by the same driver as the one on the original Beagle boards. However, they differ by the address.

- Any hardware revision differences.

- Name of the driver the hardware uses. This is often specified as a compatible attribute.

- Hardware resources such as interrupts and DMA resources used.

- Register settings specific to the hardware.

The device tree information depends on the driver using it. There can be other attributes such as GPIOs to enable functions.

Like building a kernel, the device tree is an advanced topic. We will go through an overview of the device tree. The device tree is described by a **Device Tree Source (DTS)** file. During the kernel compilation, the DTS file is compiled into a **Device Tree Blob (DTB)** or binary. The compiler used to generate a DTB is the `dtc`. It is a part of the kernel tree. It is described at `Documentation/devicetree` in the kernel tree. The device tree is often built as part of the kernel build process.

Most device tree source files are found at `arch/arm/boot/dts`. The compiled DTB files can be explicitly loaded by the bootloader or can be included as part of the kernel binary. For example, the `zImage` format used by the newer Debian/Ubuntu distributions includes the DTB files.

The concept of a device tree for the ARM architecture is relatively new. Device trees were introduced roughly at the same time frame as the introduction of the BeagleBone Black. A consequence of this is that the device tree support is still being phased in and is subject to change. Prior to the device tree, the hardware was largely described by a C source file known as a board file. This file is compiled into the kernel. Both the changes and phase-in period means that a lot of the older online tutorials for driver addition are obsolete. Another unfortunate consequence of this is that the device drivers that have not been updated for device tree support may not be available.

Pinmuxing on the BeagleBone

Pinmuxing is a combined software and hardware concept that embedded users, such as the BeagleBone users, must be very aware of if they are using anything other than the basic functions of the BeagleBone. Any interfacing using the expansion connector P8 and P9 is likely to involve the pinmux unless the hardware being interfaced matches the default settings. Some of the off-the-shelf expansion boards come with configuration settings to automate this process. Regardless of whether it is automated, it is a good idea to at least confirm the pinmux settings. As described in *Chapter 7, Interfacing with the BeagleBone*, pinmux is used to select one of the eight functions on each signal from the SoC. It is the last part of the SoC before a signal leaves and the first part before a signal enters the SoC.

From a software standpoint, it is possible for the kernel driver to be configured perfectly and yet any external connected hardware to the SoC would not work. The pinmux is controlled by a different driver. Unless the pinmux driver is configured properly, signals cannot get to or from the hardware block. This can be compared to a drawbridge between the inside of the SoC and the outside world; until the drawbridge is lowered, signals cannot get in or out. The pinmux documentation is divided between two documents on the SoC. The most reliable way to locate the documentation for the SoC and any other tools referred to from Texas Instruments is to search for the SoC family, AM335x, on its website (http://www.ti.com/). The specific links often change. The following are a few of the several tools that can be used to figure out the pinmuxing:

- Texas Instruments, which makes the SoC used on the BeagleBone, provides a pinmux tool. This is a tool for the SoC and is not specific to the BeagleBone. You will need to determine the available signals from the BeagleBone SRM or the BeagleBone schematics.

- The BeagleBoard community has a variety of tools that help to figure out the pinmux settings on all the members of the BeagleBoards. They are provided by users and are useful to vary the degree. To find them, search pinmux and BeagleBone on a search engine. The author has not used these tools and cannot comment on their usefulness.

- You can manually correlate the different documentation. The steps for these will be discussed in the next section.

Figuring out the pinmux on the BeagleBone

The process of figuring out the pinmux can be very confusing for a new user. What is described here is an attempt to identify the information from different sources and connect them to determine a pinmux setting. There are four documents that contain relevant information. They are as follows:

- **BeagleBone SRM**: This describes the signals from the SoC that are exposed on the expansion connectors, P8 and P9. Most users will start here to identify the pins they are using.

- **BeagleBone schematics**: While not strictly needed, the schematics can help clarify some signals. Some signals on the BeagleBone are connected together for backward compatibility with older revisions of the board. The schematic along with the SRM will help you identify them.

- **AM335x datasheet**: This is the documentation labeled as the datasheet on the Texas Instruments website. It is a much smaller PDF document than the TRM. Most of the information here is hardware-specific but we need it to identify the modes.

- **AM335x TRM**: This is the larger of the two documents from the Texas Instruments website. It contains the software details for programming the chip.

The process to determine the pinmux settings is as follows:

1. Using the BeagleBone SRM, identify the pins on the expansion connector you would like to use. For example, if you have an LED hooked up to pin 30 on P8, the SRM calls this GPIO2_25 and the signal is hooked up to R6 on the SoC.

2. All current versions of the BeagleBone use the ZCZ package. You can confirm this by looking at the BeagleBone schematics.

3. Search in the AM335x datasheet for what it describes as ball R6 on the ZCZ package. The datasheet is the smaller one of the two documents from the Texas Instruments website. This should be a row in a table with a column for the pin name than another column showing eight possible modes. We can ignore the electrical details for now. The eight possible modes are the eight possible functions that can be assigned to this pin or ball. The name in the pin name column can be different from the name used in the BeagleBone SRM. The two bits of information we need from this step is the name it uses here and the mode number for the function we need. In our example, the name is LCD_AC_BIAS_EN and the mode for GPIO2_25 is mode 7.

4. The AM335x SoC TRM document contains the rest of the information needed. This is the larger of the two documents. In the TRM, look for the *Control Module* chapter. Within that chapter, we get the following information:

    ○ Under the pad control registers, there is a description of the registers. It shows the bits used to control the functions. Each pin will have one such register. Refer to this to figure out the value needed for the register.

    ○ Toward the end of the chapter, there will be a list of registers. It will be in the part of the chapter labeled *Registers*. The list will show an offset and an acronym. To determine the offset, look for the pin name. It will have `conf_` prepended to it. In our example, we will look for `conf_lcd_ac_bias_en`. From the table, it shows an offset of 8ECh or 0x8EC.

From the preceding procedure, we have determined a register offset and a value. To make use of that in a current as of writing kernel, we need to get that information into the device tree. Typically, the device tree can be found at `arch/arm/boot` in the Linux kernel source tree. The exact section of the device tree will depend on the particular driver and version of the kernel. Most pinmux settings will be defined in a section similar to this:

```
pinctrl-single,pins = <
            0xEC (PIN_OUTPUT_PULLDOWN | MUX_MODE7) /* lcd_ac_bias_
en.gpio2_25 */                 >;
```

The `0xEC` value is the offset. The device tree wants the offset to be relative at the beginning of the pinmux registers. To determine the offset for the device tree from the offset from the TRM, subtract `0x800`. The next argument is the settings for the pinmux. It can be given symbolically like the example or can be given as another number. The number can be determined from the TRM's *Control Module* chapter as shown in step 4 of the preceding process.

> For readers who are familiar with direct access, all these offsets may be confusing. The pinmux register resides at a fixed physical address on the processor. The fixed physical address can be determined by looking at the TRM. The *Memory map* chapter provides the addresses of the entire SoC. From that chapter, we can see that the control module registers begin at `0x44e10000`. In the *Control Module* chapter, we can see that the pinmux or pad configuration registers begin at `0x800`. In our example, the offset for the register is at `0x8ec`. To get the full physical address add `0x44e10000` to `0x8ec` to give us `0x44e108ec`.

It is customary to note the name and function as a comment to the pinmux setting. The naming convention used is the pin name as found in the datasheet followed by a period and then followed by the function name used. The datasheet pin name is usually the pin's mode 0 function.

The BeagleBone and real-time performance

New users that are not from Linux-based embedded backgrounds often have an expectation of real-time performance. Linux is not **a real-time operating system (RTOS)**. It is beyond the scope of this book to fully address this point but some clarification of potential confusion is needed.

Real-time performance means repeatable and predictable timing behavior. It does not mean higher performance as the name would suggest. Real-time performance is often needed in embedded devices so they can respond to external events in a timely manner. For example, maintaining a consistent motor speed from a BeagleBone requires the BeagleBone to respond to the motor speed measurements in a consistent manner.

On the BeagleBone systems running Linux, real-time behavior can be addressed in the following ways for noncritical systems:

- Compared to many smaller embedded systems, the BeagleBone is considerably faster. This may be enough to approximate the real time for most of the time. It is essential to note this is viable for noncritical systems, that is, a system where an occasional violation of timing behavior does not result in something very bad.

- Modify the kernel with a real-time patched kernel. This can be very tricky to debug and provides limited real-time capabilities. Real-time patches are under development and may be buggy. This option should be considered with an understanding that considerable debugging of the kernel may be needed. There are two main variants of adding real-time behavior to the Linux kernel, as follows:

  ° Linux is modified so different parts of the kernel cannot monopolize the system for large periods of time.

  ° Linux runs as a subsystem on top of a larger real-time system. The underlying real-time system will run Linux whenever there is nothing more time critical to run.

- Leverage the PRUSS block on the BeagleBone. The PRUSS block is part of the AM335x SoC that consists of additional cores to provide real-time capabilities.

- Depending on the behavior needed, it may be possible to offload the real-time aspects to a dedicated hardware on the AM335x SoC. For example, generation of **Pulse Width Modulation (PWM)** signals can be directly done by dedicated hardware on the SoC itself.

- A complicated option is to add an external microcontroller to perform and interface it to the BeagleBone over I2C or SPI. This is similar to the last option with the PRUSS except the processing is external to the SoC.

There are a few indirect pitfalls of attempting it real time on the BeagleBone:

- Real time is not faster. Implementations requiring faster behavior without a need to guarantee timing can be improved by moving appropriate pieces to the kernel if it hasn't been done. GPIO toggling like we did for the LED exercises is slow. We did the exercises in user mode using a scripting language. Moving the code into the kernel will improve the performance.

- Merely moving into the kernel mode does not necessarily provide real-time performance. Kernel mode lacks the performance impact of many of the abstractions but other parts of the kernel can interfere with timing.

There are many more factors to consider regarding real-time behavior. This section is here mainly to clarify some confusion seen in the BeagleBoard community regarding real-time behavior. It is not intended to be anywhere near a complete overview of real-time behavior on a BeagleBone.

Summary

In this chapter, we looked at several advanced software topics. We began by looking at programming the BeagleBone like a desktop system using the C and Linux APIs. You learned that the BeagleBone shares many things with a desktop Linux system and can reuse most libraries and software developed on the desktop. However, leveraging desktop-developed software may have some potential issues on the BeagleBone. Despite the potential issues, a desktop can prototype applications with a few caveats.

We then looked at software compilation for the BeagleBone. Next, we looked at the native compilation on the BeagleBone, which works just like a desktop. However, this process can be slower compared to a desktop. We also looked at the concept of cross compiling where we compiled software for the BeagleBone on the desktop. Cross compiling is faster but there can be complications.

As an example of building software, we built a C version of Hello, World for the BeagleBone in two ways. First, we natively compiled the Hello, World application using native compilation on the BeagleBone. Then, we looked at cross compiling the same Hello, World application.

You learned that Linux has a user mode and a kernel mode and each mode has different levels of access. Due to the different levels of access, hardware support should be given through the kernel despite the tempting user-mode debugging APIs.

Next, we looked at the device tree data structure used for hardware support in the Linux kernel. We finished off the chapter with a description of the pinmux along with how to determine the configuration of the pinmux.

Finally, we rounded off the chapter with some clarification of the real-time behavior and the BeagleBone running Linux. Linux is not a real-time system.

With the topics covered in this chapter, you should be able to get a sense of what is needed software-wise to support additional hardware interfaced to the BeagleBone using the expansion connectors P8 and P9. These topics are presented largely as a roadmap to these advanced topics instead of purely as a how-to for the advanced topics.

In the next chapter, we will look at off-the-shelf expansion options for the BeagleBone, such as what the SRM describes as a *cape*, along with USB expansion options.

9
Expansion Boards and Options

We have previously looked at interfacing the custom hardware to the BeagleBone using the GPIO, SPI, and I2C interfaces. While that offers the most flexibility, there are prebuilt, off-the-shelf expansion options for the BeagleBone. These can be a quicker and a simpler way of adding features provided they meet your needs. These options provide a vast library of hardware for the BeagleBone. In this chapter, we will look at the following topics:

- Prebuilt expansion boards
- Example cape offerings
- Configuring Linux for capes
- USB expansion options
- USB versus capes for expansion
- Custom hardware versus off-the-shelf hardware

The BeagleBone capes

Capes are expansion boards that plug in to the expansion connectors, P8 and P9, on the BeagleBone and have a specific pin usage. Capes are defined in the BeagleBone SRM document. Capes are specific to the BeagleBone subfamily and specifically do not include the BeagleBoard Classic or the BeagleBoard xM. Anyone can build a cape using the description in the SRM.

 For readers familiar with the microcontroller-based Arduino boards, capes are conceptually similar to a shield for Arduino boards.

As defined in the BeagleBone SRM, capes can be of any shape, but the location of the Ethernet RJ45 connector along with the location of the LED can dictate a specific cut-out pattern. Alternatively, extra tall connectors can be used to clear the Ethernet RJ45 connector. Up to four capes can be stacked using dual-sided connectors. A dual-sided connector is a through hole connector with male pins on one side to fit the expansion connectors P8 and P9, and a female socket on the other side. However, you will need to be careful not to stack capes that electrically conflict or have conflicting resource requirements.

The main distinguishing and required feature for a cape is an I2C EEPROM used to identify the cape along with the resources it uses. The I2C EEPROM format is defined in the SRM. The exception to the EEPROM requirement is for passive expansion boards such as a blank breadboard. In order to allow stacking, the EEPROM's I2C address needs to be physically configurable to one of the four possible addresses with a dip switch or jumpers. This EEPROM is the same as the BeagleBone identification EEPROM we discussed in the exercises of the previous chapters. The specifications of EEPROM are as follows:

- 24C256 or compatible
- 32 KB
- Configurable for I2C addresses 0x54 to 0x57 (these addresses are dedicated to cape identification)
- Connected to I2C2 on P9 using pins 19 and 20

> Unless otherwise specified, the I2C bus numbers in this chapter refer to the physical bus numbers used in the schematics. Due to the way the Linux software is configured by default, physical I2C1 is not enabled. The Linux kernel numbers the buses as they are enabled. As a result, the software I2C1 is really the I2C2 bus shown in the hardware documentation.

The EEPROM contents are shown in the following table:

Name	Offset	Size	Description
Header	0	4	This contains the bytes 0xaa, 0x55, 0x33, and 0xee to identify this as a cape ID EEPROM.
Revision	4	2	This is the revision of the EEPROM format and not the revision of the cape.

Name	Offset	Size	Description
Board name	6	32	This name in ASCII text of the cape.
Version	38	4	This is the hardware version of the cape in ASCII.
Manufacture	42	16	This is the name of the cape manufacture in ASCII.
Part number	58	16	This is the part number in ASCII.
Number of pins	74	2	This is the number of pins used by the cape and the value is in hex.
Serial number	76	12	See BeagleBone SRM for description of the format.
Pin usage	88	148	These are the two bytes to describe each of the configurable pins on the BeagleBone. This is the data used to describe the pinmux setting needed for the cape. See the SRM for the details.
VDD_3V3B current	236	2	This is the maximum current in milliamp drawn from this rail. Its value is stored in hex.
VDD_5V current	238	2	This is the maximum current in milliamp drawn from this rail. Its value is stored in hex.
SYS_5V current	240	2	This is the maximum current in milliamp drawn from this rail. Its value is stored in hex.
DC supplied	242	2	If the cape supplies power like a power supply or battery cape, this field describes the current capacity of the supply.

Note that the only description of functionality in the EEPROM is the name of the name field. It is entirely up to the software to map the part number and revision fields to the appropriate functionality. The main goal of the EEPROM is to identify electrical requirements.

Capes on the BBB versus BBW

The differences between the BBB and the BBW impose a few differences in which capes will work. The BBW has an additional connector to use the onboard battery charger and LED driver. This connector has been replaced by a simpler but unpopulated set of pads with only the onboard battery charger signals at a slightly different location. Any capes that depend on that will not work on the BBB or vice versa.

Additional features on the BBB, such as the onboard flash and the video output, looks like a virtual cape to software. While the virtual capes can be disabled in software, the presence of the onboard hardware can interfere with certain capes. Resources that may conflict are as follows:

- **Onboard flash**: The onboard flash is connected to the MMC interface. The MMC interface uses signals on the expansion connector. In order to reuse those signals, the onboard flash needs to be held in reset through a combination of software and hardware signals. Refer to the BeagleBone SRM for the specific sequence required. Even with the onboard flash held in reset, these signals may need to be qualified with reset due to the processor switching the configuration to defaults at reset. Another potential complication is that SoC will probe for the onboard flash each time the BeagleBone is reset. This can interfere with the hardware using those pins. This can be worked around by forcing the boot configuration as described in the SRM.

 Any capes or expansion boards that use the pins shared with the onboard flash should not electrically drive the signals till the software has properly configured the system.

- **Onboard video**: Most complications from the onboard video are in the form of electrical loading. This can limit the speed of any signals on the video lines. In addition, the onboard video is configured for 16-bit video, which can conflict with other video usages such as 24-bit LCDs.

- **Boot order**: Capes that attempt to modify the boot order may not have the same effect on both the BBW and the BBB. The onboard flash of the BBB can change how the SoC will boot the BeagleBone.

Example capes

Capes cover a wide range of expansion hardware for the BeagleBone. There is no complete authoritative list. The Beagle board website at http://www.beagleboard. org/ lists some of the many offerings. A quick survey of what's available at the time of writing this book includes the following:

- LCD capes with a range of sizes along with different options for touch screens

- FPGA interfaces for prototyping

- Stepper motor interfaces

- Sensor capes to sense temperature, pressure, humidity, acceleration, rotation, and so on

- Wireless interface capes providing things such as Wi-Fi and Zig Bee
- 3D printer control capes
- GPS interfaces

 Cape availability will vary. This is not an exhaustive list! Features and availability are entirely up to the suppliers/designers of the cape.

Capes and software on the BeagleBone

The original design of capes is to allow automated configuration when a cape is connected to the BeagleBone. This is done by the following actions:

- The Linux kernel on boot up scans for the identification EEPROM at addresses `0x54-0x57` on I2C2

 Most kernels will refer to the hardware I2C2 bus for capes as I2C1. Keep this in mind while reading the software documentation for capes.

- If the EEPROM is found, the contents are validated
- Assuming the contents are valid, the pin configuration information is used to configure the pinmux; the appropriate drivers will be enabled

With the introduction of the device tree, the process is slightly modified. Prior to the device tree, each kernel binary supported a limited subset of capes. Newer capes that require specific initialization would require a new kernel binary. With the introduction of the device tree, it can be as simple as defining a new device tree entry. The cape system with device tree requires an additional software component, a **cape manager**. The cape manager performs the following actions:

- Scan the hardware I2C2 bus for an EEPROM at addresses `0x54` to `0x57`
- Validate the EEPROM
- Use the `PART-NUMBER:REVISION` information from the EEPROM to configure the board

The cape manager uses the device tree overlays, which is a method to graft additional information onto a running kernel's device tree. The full format and functionality are described in *Documentation/device* tree in a kernel tree. A device tree overlay has a similar syntax to a normal device. The difference is that the overlay contains only a fragment of the device tree. It is compiled using the same tools as a normal device tree file provided the tool is from a device tree overlay-enabled kernel.

An additional functionality of the cape manager is to allow the cape detection process to be overridden. Capes can be forced enabled or disabled via options passed through the Linux kernel command line. This is especially useful on the BeagleBone Black where the extra features such as the onboard flash and the video interface appear as a virtual cape. For situations on the BBB where those extra features are undesirable due to resource conflicts, the software conflicts can be eliminated by disabling them through the cape manager.

If you ever need to change the Linux kernel command line, this can be done by modifying a text file located in the first partition of the microSD card or the first partition of the onboard flash. For most versions of the bootloader, U-Boot, the kernel command line is stored in a text file named uEnv.txt. This is a text file containing the settings for the bootloader. The specifics will depend on the distribution. The changes in this file can render the BeagleBone unbootable or lead to subtle problems.

USB devices on the BeagleBone

The BeagleBone offers a USB host port that allows most USB devices supported by the Linux software to work on the BeagleBone. Many USB devices can be shared with a desktop system or used to exchange data with a desktop system. Consider the following points before using the USB option:

- **Power**: The BeagleBone can provide up to 500mA on the USB port, but it needs to be powered from the barrel connector for reliable operation. Powering the BeagleBone using the USB option may work but this is outside of the USB specification. Keep in mind the 500mA limit is a USB 2.0 specification, but some mass-marketed USB devices may rely on the 500mA limit to be unenforced.

- **Speed**: The USB port on the BeagleBone is a USB 2.0 high-speed port and can support high-speed, full-speed, and low-speed devices. However, due to the way the software and hardware is designed, high-speed devices may not archive the same throughput as a desktop system.

- **Multimedia**: USB multimedia devices such as cameras, audio interfaces, and video capture interfaces may not work well simultaneously. On many desktop systems, there are multiple USB buses each capable of the full bus speed. However, on the BeagleBone, there is only one bus. The addition of a USB hub to increase the number of ports will divide the bus capacity among all the devices.

You can see the locations of the USB host interface (at the left-hand side) and the USB device interface (at the right-hand side under the highlighted area below the LEDs) in the following image:

It is important to note the BeagleBone comes with both a USB device and a USB host interface. A USB device interface allows the BeagleBone to connect to a PC. This is the smaller mini-B connector located underneath the LEDs next to the Ethernet RJ45 connector. For many readers, this is the way the BeagleBone has been powered and used for the exercises. A USB host interface allows the BeagleBone to connect to other devices and is the focus of the discussion here. The USB host interface is the larger **A** connector located on the opposite end from the Ethernet RJ45 connector. Refer to the preceding image for the locations of each one. A simple way to remember the host versus device interfaces is to look at a USB thumb drive. A USB thumb drive is a USB device and it plugs into a USB host connector. The USB thumb drive does not fit the smaller USB device mini-B connector.

While the BeagleBone provides a single USB host port, it is possible to connect multiple USB devices to the BeagleBone via a USB hub. USB hubs come in self-powered and bus-powered types. A self-powered USB hub has a power connector to feed power. The bus-power version draws all of its power from the BeagleBone. The consequence of this is that the bus-powered version can only provide each device with a maximum of 100mA on each power, whereas the self-powered version can potentially supply up to 500mA on each power. A USB thumb drive may not need more than 100mA, but if you are interfacing a USB Wi-Fi interface along with another USB device, you are likely to need more than 100mA.

Using a self-powered USB hub along with powering the BeagleBone with the barrel can create a mess of wires. One way of working around this is to draw power for the BeagleBone from the USB hub. The USB specification does not permit this configuration as any device drawing more than 100mA should explicitly ask permission. However, some hubs do not enforce this part of the specification. The BeagleBone can be powered using such a hub and then using a USB to barrel connector adapter cable. There is no generic name for this but what you are looking for is a cable that wires pins 1 and 4 on a USB A connector to the parts of a plug that mate with the barrel connector. Keep in mind the center pin is positive.

An important aspect of a USB hub to remember is that the hub does not create additional transfer capacity. A hub connected to the BeagleBone will divide the single port's transfer capacity among all the connected devices. Connecting multiple high transfer capacity or bandwidth devices such as a USB camera may not work as well as expected. Even connecting a storage device along with a high bandwidth device may have problems if both devices are in use. For example, attempting to record video from a USB camera onto a USB thumb drive may not work well.

USB versus capes for expansion

USB and capes both offer off-the-shelf options to add functionality to the BeagleBone. There are advantages and disadvantages of each option.

The advantages of the USB option are as follows:

- They are often mass produced for the desktop/laptop market. As a high volume product, this can be obtained at a lower cost.

- USB devices are designed with power management in mind, and compliant devices have limits on power consumption.

- Since USB devices are often used for the mass market, they are often better tested so less time is spent on debugging the hardware. In practice, this can vary depending on the manufacturer of the device. At the very least, a USB device can be verified by moving it temporarily to a desktop.

- USB devices have standard functionality that the Linux kernel will recognize without a special driver. For example, all keyboards, mouse, and mass storage devices are handled in a well-known manner. This makes it simple to swap devices within the same category for other reasons such as mechanical form factor. For example, a system requiring a keyboard can be tested with a USB keyboard. Later on it can be swapped with a physically smaller USB keyboard and there is a reasonable assurance that it will just work.

- USB device support can come from the wide Linux community providing drivers.
- USB devices can be plugged in after the BeagleBone is running.

The advantages of a cape are as follows:

- Capes are designed for the BeagleBone family and have been tested to work with at least one member of the BeagleBone family.
- Capes provide the expansion option needed by the BeagleBone user, not just things wanted by the mass market. This can provide hardware that is normally not interesting enough for the high-volume, consumer-oriented market for USB devices.
- Capes can supply or consume power. A battery cape can power the BeagleBone.
- Due to the location of the expansion connectors on the BeagleBone, capes can result in a mechanically smaller package.
- Capes provide access to the I2C/SPI buses. This can help prototype by having the same chips as a final product that integrates everything into a single board.
- Capes have access to interfaces not available through USB. For example, the video interface and the general purpose memory bus is only available on the expansion connectors.
- Capes are often better documented. Schematics and the parts used are well known.
- Up to four capes can be stacked provided they do not have conflicting resource requirements.

The disadvantages of USB on the BeagleBone are as follows:

- The USB specification provides up to 500mA. Higher current devices such as some USB hard drives cheat by requiring two USB ports with a Y cable. On a BeagleBone, this requires a self-powered hub.
- Only one USB device can be connected unless a hub is used.
- All connected USB devices share the same bandwidth when a USB hub is used.
- USB devices are typically limited to mass-marketed devices of interest to consumers.

- Due to the high volume and often non-Linux targeted nature of USB devices, USB devices may be discontinued or modified without notice. Worse yet, the device may be redesigned without notice in a manner that does not work with Linux. The same model purchased today may have a totally different and incompatible design than the same model purchased tomorrow. This is important if a device needs to be replaced or reproduced.

 A redesigned device can be incompatible because most devices are mass marketed to the non-Linux market such as for Windows users. Windows users can update their drivers to support the newer design, but Linux users on desktops and on the BeagleBone do not have that option because the manufacturer may not directly support Linux users.

- USB devices are often not documented with sufficient technical details, and schematics are usually not available.
- Not all USB devices work with Linux.
- USB devices require a 5V source. SoC and most of the BeagleBone runs at 3.3V or lower. While outside of the specifications of the BeagleBone, it is possible to modify the BeagleBone to run from a lower voltage source. However, using a USB device requires a 5V source.

The disadvantages of capes are as follows:

- Capes are generally low-volume products, which can be more expensive compared to, if available, a USB version of the same functionality.
- Capes may not be interchangeable between the BeagleBone White and BeagleBone Black versions. Capes originally designed for the BBW may require additional software work to use on the BBB. The additional features such as the onboard flash and video interfaces may conflict with capes. For example, LCD capes can require video timings that are incompatible with the video interface.
- The physical cape interface over the P9 and P8 connector is not electrically protected. Most of the signals are directly connected to SoC. In contrast, the USB port is designed with a certain level of protection. Excess power draw will generate a fault on USB; whereas, the same excess power draw can damage the BeagleBone.
- Capes cannot be hot swapped.
- Cape support may not be functional in all versions of the Linux kernel. The cape manager software at the time of writing this book has not merged into the main line Linux kernel.

- Power management support can vary greatly among different capes. There is no requirement to handle power management on a cape.

The advantages and disadvantages of capes versus USB can help eliminate options but sometimes that does not provide a clear picture. Consider a BeagleBone configured to stream video from a camera over the network. If we solely look at the advantages of USB, a camera and a USB Wi-Fi interface will be the cheapest. Most modern USB cameras provide a standard USB interface that uses generic drivers, namely, the **USB Video Class (UVC)** driver. However, if the entire system is considered, the USB bus may not have enough bandwidth to accommodate video data coming from the camera and video being sent over the Wi-Fi interface. A refinement of this is to consider a combination of capes and USB. There are more USB camera options than there are cape camera options, so that would make USB the best option for cameras. A Wi-Fi cape does not share the bandwidth with the USB so that solves that problem. In addition, this avoids the problem of locating a Linux-compatible USB Wi-Fi interface.

Custom hardware versus off-the-shelf hardware

For requirements not provided by an existing cape or a USB device, the only option available is to build custom hardware. However, for requirements that may appear to be available in either a cape form or a USB form, the choice is less clear. Many capes were created because of requirements that cannot be fulfilled with off-the-shelf hardware. For all of these options, some expertise in hardware design is needed. You can learn it or can seek out services. Here are a few considerations and things that should be done:

- Existing off-the-shelf hardware can be modified. Capes often provide schematics and sometimes the designers are available for consultation. For this to be feasible, the existing hardware should be somewhat close to what is needed. For example, if you need the BeagleBone interfaced to a chip with a large number of connections, it does not make sense to start with anything other than a cape or a USB device with at least that chip. Things to consider with these options are as follows:
    - The necessary signals are available. It should not be buried under a **Ball Grid Array (BGA)** or other hard to access points.
    - The necessary signals need to be accessible. The difference between this and the last point is this point refers to the circuit board, for example, a multilayered circuit board can hide a lot of things.

○ The starting point should be as close as possible to the final point. Many devices have configuration options that may require the board to be wired up in a way specific to that option. Starting with a board that has different options can introduce additional complexities that may make this moot.

- Capes often provide only one function. If multiple functions are needed and they are all available as separate capes, stacking is an option but this could mean the entire stack taking up a lot of room. Depending on the type of cape, stacking can also cause electrical issues if there are any fast signals in the entire stack.

- If the end goal is to prototype a product, it can make sense to build a custom board. Depending on community interest, adding EEPROM can turn this into a cape.

- A custom interface board is likely to require Linux kernel software work. Available capes often come with software configuration information. This can be an added burden if you don't have any expertise in those areas.

- Even if modification of an existing cape is impractical, many capes are open hardware designs that can be leveraged to produce your own version. Please verify the licenses are compatible with your goals before doing so.

- Even if the functionality you need is available as a USB device, building a custom board can be a better choice. USB devices are generally mass-marketed products that may be revised or discontinued without notice. In addition, USB power management relies on the entire USB stack working correctly. Moving to a non-USB option, if available, can simplify power management and give you control over the hardware design. Non-USB power management can be as simple as toggling a GPIO signal or sending a command over an I2C/SPI control channel.

- If the custom expansion board is chosen, there may be added software support requirements. Each time the system is updated with a newer version of the distribution, the same software changes will have to be made. This can entail porting the software if the software interface used has been changed. One way of addressing this is to attempt to get your software changes committed to the source. This is known as upstreaming. The full process of upstreaming is beyond the scope of this book. Steps to upstream your software changes, such as a new driver for the kernel, are as follows:

  1. Make sure your changes are against the current development version of the kernel.

  2. Subscribe to the discussion list for the relevant subsystems your driver uses.

3. Be sure the software is written in a manner consistent with the kernel; this includes white space format. Refer to *Documentation/Coding-Style* in the kernel source tree for details. This step is often a major stumbling block for new submissions.

4. Break up your changes into logical blocks that add or remove a specific functionality.

5. Submit the blocks as a series of unified diffs to the discussion list for comments. Do not use attachments. Act on the comments and iterate if needed.

6. If successful, upstreaming can reduce the support overhead with custom expansion boards.

7. Keep in mind the difference between a custom expansion board and a cape is largely the EEPROM. It may be useful to others.

- A very important determining factor is resource constraints on the expansion connector. Some signals may be available only on certain pins. Those pins may have been specified to be used as a cape or be used by another cape. If that is the only way to connect the combination of hardware, then you have no choice other than to build a custom expansion board. For example, if the combination of interfaces used on the expansion connector forces you to pins 19 and 20 on P9 as something other than I2C, you cannot have a cape.

Summary

In this chapter, we looked at some of the off-the-shelf options of the BeagleBone expansion. This hardware library comes in two general versions, a USB-based version, and something known as capes. This chapter introduced a lot of off-the-shelf interfacing details.

For capes, the specification is provided in the SRM. The main differentiator for a cape is the identification of EEPROM. This EEPROM identifies hardware resources the cape uses, such as pinmux configuration and electrical requirements. An important detail is that EEPROM does not define software requirements such as drivers. The current software at the time of writing this book uses a cape manager to configure capes. A cape manager associates the cape with a device tree overlay to describe the hardware on the cape to the software. On the BeagleBone Black, new features unique to it appear to the software as a virtual cape.

Another off-the-shelf expansion option is a USB device. USB devices are often mass-marketed devices, which can be lower in cost but may have issues for embedded uses like on the BeagleBone. Choosing between USB and cape expansion options requires an understanding of the limitations on each interface. Using a combination of both USB and a cape can be a good idea.

We also looked at the reasons for a custom expansion board. We compared off-the-shelf options such as a cape or USB with a custom expansion board. An important detail to keep in mind is that all capes are just a subset of an expansion board with specific pin usage on the expansion connector along with EEPROM requirements.

In this book, we have covered the BeagleBone basic starting from unboxing your BeagleBone to programming your BeagleBone, along with expanding your BeagleBone for interconnectivity and other purposes. Along the way, we covered the basic recovery procedures in case of mistakes. Now that you have a foundation, go forth and build your embedded device with a BeagleBone!

A
The Boot Process

The BBB/BBW boards offer several ways of booting that can be leveraged for different purposes, such as recovering a board from a software corruption, putting a used board into a known state, or booting a newly-built board. This appendix provides an overview of what is possible, as this subject does come up in various forms on the support forums and mailing lists. For complete details, refer to the AM335x technical reference manual available at http://www.ti.com. We will cover the following topics:

- What happens when the power is switched on
- Getting an initial bootloader running
- Getting the main bootloader
- Linux and beyond
- Potential alternative boot uses

What happens when the power is turned on

Unlike simple processors where the user's code executes immediately at power on, the AM335x processors feature an internal ROM to offer a variety of choices to start the system. At power on, the internal ROM starts running and looks at the SYSBOOT signals connected to the processor to decide whether to load the user code and to configure the device containing the user code appropriately. The BBB exposes a subset of the available options; this subset can be selected by the user button.

Note that the user button is only checked on power up (not reset!). In the following image, the user button is highlighted. Since the BBW does not have an onboard flash, there is no user button.

Bootloader

Bootloader is the part of the system responsible for loading the operating system. This is similar to the concept of BIOS on desktop systems. By default, if the user button is not depressed, the processor will attempt to boot from the onboard flash on the BBB. The processor will configure the flash to access and look for a special file called MLO on the first partition. The MLO file contains a first stage bootloader along with a checksum to let the ROM know that it is valid code. If the checksum is valid, the contents are copied to the internal memory and the processor will attempt to execute from there. The first stage bootloader's size is limited by the size of the internal memory.

The job of the first stage bootloader is to configure the external (DDR2/DDR3) memory and read in the second stage bootloader into the external memory and pass control. On a standard BBB system, this will load u-boot.img from the same location as MLO. The u-boot.img file is the main code for U-Boot—the main bootloader.

Once U-Boot is running, it will configure additional hardware as needed. On a standard system, it will attempt to load a configuration defined by u-env.txt in the same partition as the rest. Using that information, it will attempt to load and start Linux from the specified media such as the onboard flash. The standard U-Boot (as shipped) will check for an external microSD card. If present, it will load the Linux kernel from there instead of the internal flash. The following flowchart shows the boot process and how it is changed by the user button:

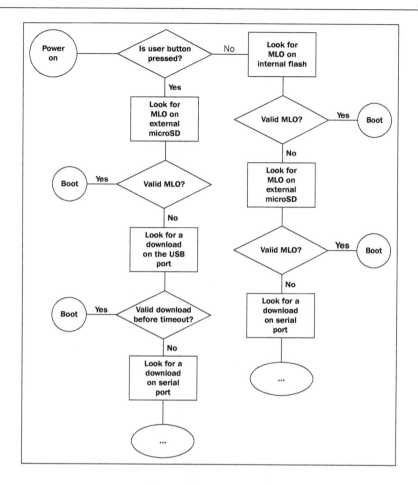

Flash memory/microSD

The internal flash memory is normally divided into two partitions:

- The first partition contains the MLO, u-env.txt, and u-boot.img files, and sometimes the Linux kernel
- The second partition contains the Linux filesystem

For a lot of projects, the second partition is the only part that is typically modified and is the partition that is most likely to be corrupted due to user errors. The first partition is not often corrupted due to user errors. From a recovery standpoint, this can be addressed as simply as inserting a configured microSD card and allowing the system to boot! For the microSD card, such as on the BBW, things are analogous as the flash memory used on the BBB is **embedded MMC (eMMC)**. eMMC is basically the same microSD card permanently mounted on the board.

On a standard system, the onboard LEDs have a pattern to indicate whether things have got as far as loading the Linux kernel. This is a function of the U-Boot configuration.

If the user button is pressed again when power is applied, the BBB will look for the same MLO file on the external microSD card. If the file is found and the checksum matches, it will attempt the same boot process as explained earlier but using the external SD card. This is useful if the bootloader itself is corrupted.

A more advanced booting method is possible if the user button is pressed at power on. The BBB is capable of downloading a bootloader over the serial port or the USB device port.

Linux and beyond

For most BBB/BBW users, the boot process ends when their application is running. However, from a support point of view, there is an earlier dividing line. What happens after the bootloader (U-Boot) has finished is often a different support process than what happens during and before the bootloader runs. The bootloader and the earlier messages are typically only visible through the debug serial port, whereas Linux messages can be accessed via USB or the Ethernet using SSH.

For most users, the bootloader starts Linux. How Linux gets started depends entirely on the bootloader configuration. For the BBB, the bootloader will load the kernel and other Linux support pieces from the microSD card (if present); failing that, it will fall back to the internal flash. For advanced Linux development such as kernel development, the kernel does not usually need to be updated on the internal eMMC flash. A microSD card can be prepared and the bootloader will load Linux from there without having to press the user button, provided a valid bootloader lives on the internal flash memory.

The exact process beyond loading the kernel is determined by the Linux distribution chosen. Depending on the revision of the BBB, this can be either Angström or Debian. Launching an application is specific to the Linux distribution and is beyond the scope of this book.

Alternative boot uses

By pressing the user button prior to power on, an external microSD card can be used to reflash a BBB to the factory state. This is useful if the flash is corrupted, if a used board is purchased, or if you want to reset a board between class sessions. Images to reflash a BBB can be downloaded at www.beagleboard.org.

More advanced uses of the alternative boot option include rapid development by allowing a desktop or laptop to preconfigure a microSD without having to wait for the image to be written to the onboard flash memory.

Summary

The boot process can be altered by pressing the user button to force booting from an external microSD card or other devices. Regardless of which device or boot media, the BBB/BBW only knows to look for MLO. The MLO file is the first member of the chain that ends with Linux running. As such, a corrupt MLO/u-boot can make the board appear dead unless the debug serial port is examined.

After going through the exercises and building an understanding of the essentials of the BeagleBone, the next step is to build on what you have learned. You can apply this knowledge on your own projects or adapt one of the many open source projects for the BeagleBone. In the course of your project, you will learn more advanced techniques as you encounter hurdles. The theory presented in this book should provide a foundation to help surmount the challenges from your own projects.

B

Terms and Definitions

New BeagleBone users come from backgrounds that vary both technically and geographically. In this appendix, we will go through some terms to help you understand this book and other BeagleBone resources such as the community mailing list:

- **Active low/active high**: These are different electrical ways of describing a signal. Active high and active low refers to the electrical state a signal is considered to be active. For example, an enable or chip select signal can be described as active high or active low. An active low enable or chip select signal means when the signal is at the electrical value 0 (usually 0V), the signal is enabled or the chip is selected. Conversely, an active high enable or chip select signal means when the signal is at the electrical value 1 (3.3V for the BeagleBone), the signal is enabled or the chip is selected. The opposite state in both cases would mean the chip is not selected. A related concept is tristating.

- **Altoids tin**: Altoids is a mint candy sold in many parts of the world. It is commonly distributed in a small metal container with rounded corners, an Altoids tin. The tin is often used to store small items and it happens to match the shape of the BeagleBone.

- **Directories**: Linux has the concept of a directory to help organize things on a storage device. On other systems, such as Mac OS or Windows, this is the equivalent of a folder. It is analogous to a physical folder.

- **Electro Static Discharge (ESD)**: Many modern electronic devices, such as the BeagleBone, are sensitive to static electricity. ESD is the damaging discharge of static electricity, which is similar to getting shocked by touching a door knob after walking across a carpet. That shock might be an annoyance for you, but for the tiny transistors inside the silicon chips, they carry enough energy to destroy microscopic structures on the transistor.

- **Hosts and targets**: These are terms used to describe a typical embedded development setup. An embedded system is often limited compared to a desktop or a laptop system. For example, embedded systems may have limited computing power, memory, connectivity, and human-oriented I/O systems such as keyboards and displays. To expedite development, a desktop or a laptop is often paired with the embedded system. The embedded system is the target, as in the target of the development, and the host system is the desktop or laptop. The BeagleBone has considerably more capability than other embedded systems, but the same terms are applicable.

- **Man pages**: This term is short for manual pages, and these are the traditional way Linux/Unix commands are documented. On most Linux systems, you can pull up a man page by going to the command prompt and using the man command, for example, man ls. This will pull up the man page for the ls command. Man pages can also be found by searching for man ls on a search engine.

- **Programmable Real-time Unit Subsystem (PRUSS)**: This is a block on the SoC used by the BeagleBone to support real-time hardware operation. The PRUSS subsystem provides two **Programmable Real-time Units (PRUs)** to support real-time operations in hardware. The main processor on the BeagleBone is an ARM Cortex-A8 and it commonly runs Linux; neither of these pieces are designed for real time. Real time means each time you do something, you can predict how long it will take and when it will happen. For example, if you were to use Linux to toggle a signal very rapidly, you will notice the signal is not always regularly timed. Similarly, there are hardware aspects of the Cortex-A8 that can make the timing not completely predictable. The PRU is an independent microcontroller designed to offload real-time tasks from Linux. On many other SoCs, the PRU equivalent would be an external microcontroller chip.

- **System on a Chip (SoC)**: This is an integrated chip that offers a processor and peripherals in a single package. The BeagleBone uses the AM3358 SoC from Texas Instruments and provides an ARM processor, memory controller, I2C controller, Ethernet controller, and more on a single package. Prior to SoCs, the same functionality required multiple chips. The AM3358 SoC is what makes the low cost of the Beagle boards and BeagleBones possible.

- **Secure Shell (SSH)**: This is an optionally encrypted network protocol used to connect to other systems for things such as command-line access. The encryption part is not essential for our use, but SSH can provide some simple level of security if the BeagleBone is ever directly connected to an unsecured network, such as the Internet. SSH also provides the basis for file transfer protocols, such as SCP or SFTP. SCP allows files to be copied to and from an SSH server such as the BeagleBone. SSH consists of a server on the device you are accessing and a client on the machine you are coming from. On Linux desktops, OpenSSH (`http://www.openssh.com/`) is a common package. For embedded devices, Dropbear (`https://matt.ucc.asn.au/dropbear/dropbear.html`) is another smaller package. Both of these packages implement the SSH server and `client.SSH`. Most BeagleBone distributions will use one of these SSH implementations. SSH clients and the related file transfer tools such as SCP exist for most systems. A sampling of SSH clients are as follows:

    - The OpenSSH package's client has been ported to many systems. This provides both SSH and SCP functionality.

    - PuTTY (`http://www.putty.org/`) is an SSH client for Windows systems.

    - WinSCP (`http://winscp.net/eng/index.php`) is an SCP client for Windows.

- **Tristate**: A tristate signal can assume one of three possible states. It can be logic 0, logic 1, or a third high impedance state. Sometimes high impedance is designated as `Hi-Z`. A high impedance state means the signal is electrically disconnected. It behaves as if nothing is connected. Using a chip select, multiple devices can be connected in parallel. As long as the chip select is inactive, each device remains in the high impedance state. The high impedance state prevents the devices from electrically fighting with each other. On the BeagleBone, the high impedance state can be simulated in most cases by configuring the signal as an input.

Index

Symbols

Thank you for buying
Learning BeagleBone

About Packt Publishing

Packt, pronounced 'packed', published its first book, *Mastering phpMyAdmin for Effective MySQL Management*, in April 2004, and subsequently continued to specialize in publishing highly focused books on specific technologies and solutions.

Our books and publications share the experiences of your fellow IT professionals in adapting and customizing today's systems, applications, and frameworks. Our solution-based books give you the knowledge and power to customize the software and technologies you're using to get the job done. Packt books are more specific and less general than the IT books you have seen in the past. Our unique business model allows us to bring you more focused information, giving you more of what you need to know, and less of what you don't.

Packt is a modern yet unique publishing company that focuses on producing quality, cutting-edge books for communities of developers, administrators, and newbies alike. For more information, please visit our website at www.packtpub.com.

About Packt Open Source

In 2010, Packt launched two new brands, Packt Open Source and Packt Enterprise, in order to continue its focus on specialization. This book is part of the Packt Open Source brand, home to books published on software built around open source licenses, and offering information to anybody from advanced developers to budding web designers. The Open Source brand also runs Packt's Open Source Royalty Scheme, by which Packt gives a royalty to each open source project about whose software a book is sold.

Writing for Packt

We welcome all inquiries from people who are interested in authoring. Book proposals should be sent to author@packtpub.com. If your book idea is still at an early stage and you would like to discuss it first before writing a formal book proposal, then please contact us; one of our commissioning editors will get in touch with you.

We're not just looking for published authors; if you have strong technical skills but no writing experience, our experienced editors can help you develop a writing career, or simply get some additional reward for your expertise.

Building a BeagleBone Black Super Cluster

ISBN: 978-1-78398-944-7   Paperback: 156 pages

Build and configure your own parallel computing Beowulf cluster using BeagleBone Black ARM systems

1. Configure your own cluster for high-speed parallel computing.

2. Benefit from your personally configured super computer which is a power efficient, low-cost, and highly scalable super computer.

3. Write your own cluster software with the help of practical examples using powerful computational libraries specifically designed for distributed memory machines.

BeagleBone for Secret Agents

ISBN: 978-1-78398-604-0   Paperback: 162 pages

Browse anonymously, communicate secretly, and create custom security solutions with open source software, the BeagleBone Black, and cryptographic hardware

1. Interface with cryptographic hardware to add security to your embedded project, securing you from external threats.

2. Use and build applications with trusted anonymity and security software such as Tor and GPG to defend your privacy and confidentiality.

3. Work with low-level I/O on BeagleBone Black such as I2C, GPIO, and serial interfaces to create custom hardware applications.

Please check **www.PacktPub.com** for information on our titles

BeagleBone Robotic Projects

ISBN: 978-1-78355-932-9 Paperback: 244 pages

Create complex and exciting robotic projects with the BeagleBone Black

1. Get to grips with robotic systems.

2. Communicate with your robot and teach it to detect and respond to its environment.

3. Develop walking, rolling, swimming, and flying robots.

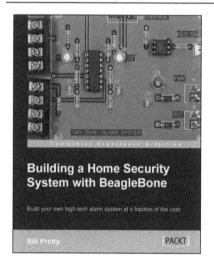

Building a Home Security System with BeagleBone

ISBN: 978-1-78355-960-2 Paperback: 120 pages

Build your own high-tech alarm system at a fraction of the cost

1. Build your own state-of-the-art security system.

2. Monitor your system from anywhere you can receive e-mail.

3. Add control of other systems such as sprinklers and gates.

4. Save thousands on monitoring and rental fees.

Please check **www.PacktPub.com** for information on our titles